Bengali Women

MULTICULTURAL
STUDENT PROGRAMS

Manisha Roy

The University
of Chicago Press

Chicago
and London

Bengali Women

**With a new
Afterword**

The University of Chicago Press, Chicago 60637
The University of Chicago Press, Ltd., London

For permission to quote from Edward C.
Dimock and Denise Levertov, editors, *In Praise
of Krishna: Songs from the Bengali,* acknowl-
edgment is made to the Asian Literature Program of the Asia Society and to Doubleday
and Co.

Library of Congress Cataloging-in-Publication Data

Roy, Manisha, 1936–
    Bengali women / Manisha Roy : with a new afterword.
      p.   cm.
    Includes bibliographical references and index.
    ISBN 0-226-73043-3 (pbk.)
      1. Women—India—West Bengal. 2. Women, Hindu—
India—West Bengal. 3. Upper classes—India—West
Bengal. I. Title.
HQ1744.B47R68 1992
305.42′0954′14—dc20   92-14268
                                             CIP

ISBN 0-226-73043-3

This book is dedicated to the memory
of my mother, Bina Roy (1918–72), a
Bengali woman of very striking
personality who did not live long
enough to see this publication.

"How I cherished to be married to Krishna! My husband turned out to be neither Krishna, nor Vishnu, but the grandson of Faringa, the buffoon weaver."

Translated from a Bengali proverb in the dialect of Mymenshing.

Contents

Foreword

"One's mother and one's motherland are superior to heaven itself."
—*Sanskrit proverb.*

"The teacher is ten times more venerable than a sub-teacher, the father a hundred times more than a teacher, but the mother a thousand times more than the father."
Manu II: 145

The venerability of the mother is no secret of the social, family, and religious life of India, especially of Bengal. One need look only at the poetry of Rabindranath Tagore, for example, to see the three-way equivalence made: mother as woman, as great goddess, and as the land of Bengal itself. In his *Amar sonar bangla* ("My Golden Bengal"), now the national anthem of Bangladesh, Tagore sings of his land as a beautiful and fertile woman, mother of all her Bengali sons, adored by them, providing them strength and succor. And of all the forms that deity takes in Bengal, the goddess—"Mother"—is most prominent. She is Umā, the child bride, the potential mother; she is Kāli, the mother in her fearsome aspect, who can take life as well as give it. She is Durgā, slayer of demons, protectress.

And not only is the goddess mother, but mother is the goddess. Those who have known Bengali matriarchs, in life or through films and novels, are prepared to believe it. For she is stern but loving, ruling the household with absolute authority, the symbols of it being the vermilion line in the part of her hair—a sign that her husband lives and a testament to her own virtue—and the bunch of keys tied to the end of her sari. An essential quality, and the primary aim, of womanhood, is motherhood. To be true to the vows to one's husband, and to be the mother of sons, is an innate virtue, the almost magical power of a woman, a power which insures the smooth functioning of the universe and by which a woman can reverse, as did Sāvitri and Behulā,[1] even the decisions of the gods.

But of course a woman is many other things. She is daughter, she is daughter-in-law, she is wife and lover, she is an old woman past the age of childbearing. She may be barren, a situation which can become truly tragic. And, of course, she is human. The pressures of society and of her emotions and physical passions work strongly on her. She is lonely and domineering, afraid and yearning, loving and terrified of love—she is like anyone, anywhere.

This is one of the major strengths of Manisha Roy's book. She shows us in its pages, through objective analysis interspersed with autobiographical accounts of sometimes terrible poignancy by Bengali women themselves, what it is to be not yet a mother, or a mother who has been. We are inclined to think of India as a "charmic society"—a society in which roles are all-important: the king is a good king, the student a good student, the mother a good mother, and all is well with the world. And we are inclined to forget that these roles are filled by individuals, with conflicts and pressures and passions of a highly personal sort, not always commensurate with the ideal. We meet some of those individuals in this book. But we are also shown the awful power of tradition, which to a large extent does dictate the role of wife and mother, being at the same time responsible for one of the major conflicts: that between the attainment of a powerful and ascetic husband like Śiva and the romance of the stories of the pretty and playful Krishna. The tensions involved, on the parts of both mother and son, in the woman's roles as mother on the one hand and mistress on the other, are considerable. Freud, in his *Three Contributions to a Psychology of Love*, made this clear. And while the traditions and conditions of Bengali society and that of the west sometimes differ widely, their effects on individuals within the two are perhaps not all that different.

One of the most significant observations in the book, it seems to me, is that of what happens to a woman when, because of her loss of fertility, she also loses power. Or, perhaps better, she seeks to transmute her former social and almost religious power of fertility into personal and spiritual power: she becomes the disciple of a *guru*. If one looks at the ancient myth of Sasthi, the goddess of child-birth and of the protection of children, one sees this borne out in an interesting way—a way which is also a comment on another of a Bengali woman's tensions, that between the mother and the daughter-in-law in her house. [2] The core story is a very simple one: the mother-in-law is to perform the worship of Sasthi, but the offerings are eaten by one of her daughters-in-law. Because of this, the girl's six sons are stolen by Sasthi. When the seventh is stolen, the girl goes before the goddess and begs for the return of her sons; the goddess agrees, but the boys refuse to go, saying that Sasthi is their true mother. The girl agrees to become a devotee of the goddess, to take instruction from her mother-in-law, and she goes home with her sons. In the myth, the mother-in-law functions as the goddess. Because she has sons, she is the repository of *shakti*, power. But her sons are grown and married. The conflict is with the young girl, who is still fertile and still exercising the natural power of childbirth. Sons are gifts of the goddess. She is their true mother, as they themselves point out. She gives them as gifts, at birth, and she gives them, or perhaps better, loans them, to their wives at marriage. The mother-son bond is never broken. But the mother-in-law is losing power, and the young girl is gaining it. She is on the verge of that psychologically and socially complex change that Manisha Roy so well describes.

I have learned much from the book. I have watched Bengali society in person and through literature for some time now, and have known some Bengali women, insofar as it is possible for a foreigner to do so. But despite such writers as Tagore, who had real respect and compassion for women, and despite many friendships and much observation, there was much I would not be told, or could not be told, or could not see. The women in this book, including the writer herself, speak very clearly, and it will be impossible for me to pick up another Bengali book without hearing their voices. Their voices are perhaps in some cases too clear, and will irritate some ears. (I myself must confess to a desire to take exception to the interpretation of medieval Vaishnavism as being debilitating; but my own prejudice speaks here, and goes against a commonly held Bengali opinion.) The study clearly cannot speak to or describe every Bengali woman everywhere. But it is honest, and in our understanding of Bengali culture and society, and as people, we are far better off because of it.

EDWARD C. DIMOCK, JR.

Preface

The subject matter of this book has been growing slowly over the years out of my own experience as both an insider and an observer of Bengali culture. I began to keep records of the human interaction among families within a section of Bengali society long before I was trained as a student of anthropology. Born of Bengali parents but brought up in a state outside Bengal, I first really encountered the city of Calcutta and its people when I entered college there at the age of fifteen. It was as an adult that I began to participate in the culture and was struck by a number of things that later turned out to be interesting from an anthropological point of view. I was struck, for instance, by the way women interacted with men and the way they talked, behaved, and expressed themselves. These observations later began to form patterns when I went back to Calcutta after four years of anthropological training in American universities. It was then that I began to record data systematically and began to see certain patterns in the way women—mostly married women—in these upper and upper middle-class families played their multiple roles vis-à-vis other roles within their joint-families. It was not until later—1970-72—when I was a student in an anthropological department with a strong emphasis on psychology that I began to see the possibility of a meaningful analysis of such patterns of behavior I had been observing all these years. It was clear that understanding must be sought at least partly in the methods of early socialization offered by a joint-family in a very distinctive religious and cultural milieu. The initial idea of using my volumes of data collected intermittently over nine years (1951-59 and 1965-69) for the purpose of an analytical research came from my then academic adviser and guide, Professor Melford E. Spiro, whose constant encouragement and help in the process of analysis made the final undertaking possible.

As a student of anthropology, I have always been interested in family dynamics and role-interactions within the family. This interest led me during 1971 to begin research on the implications of changing role-interactions within American marriages of today. With the decision to shift the research to Bengal, I became keenly aware of a need for a clear understanding of factors and forces underlying role-interactions within one given culture in order to develop a cross-cultural method of investigation. My involvement with the nuances of human interaction within a Bengali family opened my eyes to many problems in studying another culture.

This book deals with Bengali women of a particular socio-economic background in urban Bengal where I conducted my research. While some of the aspects of observation regarding social, cultural, and psychological factors observed in this section of Bengali society may very well be found within similar socio-economic sections of other parts of India, without further anthropological study I am unable to draw any conclusions. My experience with other parts of India and my detailed discussions with other Indian scholars from outside Bengal, however, lead me to believe that most of what I observed in Bengal may be similar elsewhere, although the genesis of frustrations because of heightened romantic expectations may be less developed in other parts of India. Be that as it may, I can only say that this book describes the life of upper-class Bengali women alone, and I cannot make any generalizations about Indian women as a whole.

The families I observed and studied closely are from the group
of upper and upper middle-class urbanized Hindu Bengalis who
share similar religious, educational, and economic backgrounds.
The term upper class will be used to refer to this rather
amorphous socio-economic group covering a fairly large category
including some families with and some without property. What is
clearly discernible in this class is that there is a homogeneous
culture shared by these families who value higher education and
salaried professions.

Although my original research was done over a period of a
decade, since I dealt with a group of women who live secluded
lives and since I concentrated on a particular age group (between
thirty and fifty) for most of my information, a somewhat static
picture emerges. Their life histories along with my own observations of younger girls supplied me with the information on early
socialization that did not seem to be effected noticeably by
external factors. No significant differences were to be noted at
that time in the behavior of the daughters and granddaughters of
my informants when I interviewed them. Taking the class as a
whole, certain changes can be discerned during the last two
decades. The most important economic factor causing this
change is the general decline in income of this class. Women
cannot remain "ladies of leisure" anymore. Many families are
educating their daughters for vocations. To be more specific, the
major changes that began to affect the life-style of the younger
generation of women came as a direct result of the political and
economic changes in West Bengal after the partition in 1947, the
impact of which was still unrealized in the lives of the older
women I studied.

Data collected during the first seven years was unsystematic
and sporadic. During the second phase (1965–69), I recorded
over fifty detailed life histories of women and the same number of
case studies with detailed information on families. These were
married women between the ages of twenty-five and fifty-five. The
average age of marriage is around nineteen and all women had
completed high school, while four had masters' degrees, fourteen
had bachelors' and seventeen had two years of college. They all
lived in joint-families with number of members ranging between
six and twelve. All women, at the time of interview, had at least
one child; some had as many as five. I interviewed women and

talked to many men informally. The woman I describe in the singular is an archetype of women in her economic, social, and cultural group. While the "she" I refer to is a construct, a portrait, the depicted activities and responses in her role are far from abstract. She will be seen in her life cycle as in the changing frames of a movie rather than in stills. Most of the descriptions of feelings and opinions that are presented are from the point of view of the informants except when I clearly insert my own observations and analysis. Case studies, which are used for examples and illustrations, are verbatim translations from the direct speech of the informants. When I use terms such as "frustrations" and "compensations," it should be remembered that these terms are mine as an anthropologist who is attempting to "translate" native feelings for wider understanding. Only a few women with college education ever used these terms in English, although this group of Bengalis use a number of English words in their colloquial Bengali. It must also be emphasized that this group of women and men are highly articulate and verbal people.

This study raises a methodological point that has been considered in some anthropological literature (E. R. Leach, 1963). Can an anthropologist understand and analyze his or her own society? M. N. Srinivas (1969) deals with the problem and shows how studying one's own culture affords both advantages and disadvantages toward scientific understanding. Srinivas argues that, even within one's own culture, a specific class, caste, or locality may provide enough foreignness and distance for a native investigator to make an entry as a relatively detached observer. Since I was born and brought up in a different state, my entry to Bengal could be considered new. Unlike most anthropologists, I followed the process in reverse. I gradually became a nonparticipant observer, having been a participating nonobserver. My being a Bengali woman no doubt influenced my observations and interactions with my informants whom I also knew as friends and neighbors. I feel that this was an advantage, constituting a source of insight that comes not from intellect alone but from empathy, a resource that both scientists and novelists need in order to understand the people they study.

I have discussed the problem of this research and the various ramifications of Bengali life and character with a number of Bengali intellectuals as well as American scholars over the years. Apart from personal experience and systematically collected data, the third and indirect source of information for the research came from Bengali literature of various kinds—newspapers, short stories, novels, and biographies. I cross-checked some of my observations and conclusions against my reading of Bengali literature as well as popular and scholarly writings in English on Bengali culture (see the bibliography).

This study began as a doctoral dissertation under the supervision of Melford E. Spiro and was submitted to the Department of Anthropology at the University of California at San Diego in 1972. Let me, at this point, take the opportunity to acknowledge my gratitude to all the women and men of Bengali society who were so generous with their time and candid expressions about their lives and feelings. I am also grateful to many friends and teachers for both their emotional and academic support at various stages of this study. Specific mention must be made of Professors F. G. Bailey and Gananath Obeyesekere of the University of California, San Diego; Professors Milton B. Singer and Ralph Nicholas of the University of Chicago; Maureen Patterson of the South Asian Library, the University of Chicago. I am specially indebted to Professors A. K. Ramanujan, Edward C. Dimock, Jr., David M. Schneider, all at the University of Chicago, and Dr. Prakash Desai, a Chicago psychiatrist, for their valuable and constructive comments on reading the first draft of the manuscript. I thank Professor Edward C. Dimock for writing the Foreword also. My friends who supported me with their consistent moral encouragement in this endeavor are too numerous to name individually. I thank them all.

I also thank the University of Colorado at Denver for its financial support toward the preparation of the manuscript, as well as Diana K. Fabrizio and Evelyn Eller for typing the final draft.

1 Introduction

This book deals with the frustrations and compensations in the life cycle of a Hindu Bengali woman in an upper and upper middle-class family in India. A woman in such a family is brought up to play a number of specific roles. Her early experience in her natal family builds up romantic fantasies and expectations that are not necessarily satisfied by those ideal roles she is expected to play in her married life. The sexual and emotional frustrations that such a woman faces in her married life are, however, partially satisfied through certain familial roles as well as one extra-familial role. The first roles that promise satisfaction but sometimes fail include those of wife and mother; other roles that offer satisfaction are as a brother's wife and, later, a guru's disciple.

This study also shows that in a social system such as a joint-family described in the following pages the familial roles within the process of the developmental cycle are adjusted to one another in such a way that psychological fulfillment remains only partial. Personality needs are generated and then in part frustrated; but to achieve any level of gratification the full array of joint-family roles is required. A system such as this must sacrifice the whole satisfaction of one individual, either on the structural or psychological level, so that other members in different roles may be at least partly satisfied.

The structural, cultural, and psychological conditions that bring on the frustrations as well as the compensations mentioned above will be discussed within the context of a woman's life cycle. To introduce the woman in her home, a sketch of Bengali culture is necessary.

Bengali Background

The state of West Bengal [1] lies at the eastern end of the Gangetic plain of northern India, skirted on the north by the Himalayan ranges and their extensive forests. Bangladesh and Assam lie to the east, the Bay of Bengal to the south, and the states of Bihar and Orissa to the west. Ecologically, Bengal has several peculiarities. The incoming monsoon track is from the southeast. The high ranges to the north and the vast tract of dense forest along the southern seafront contribute to the high rainfall of the monsoon from June to September, flooding the streets of Calcutta and the rivers in the countryside. These heavy rains encourage a high yield of jute, tea, and rice. Not counting the Himalayan high ranges on the north and the tableland of South Bihar near the western border, Bengal is a vast alluvial plain intersected and enriched by a remarkable network of rivers and bodies of water. These lakes and waterways play a significant role not only in Bengal's economy (making possible a self-sufficient jute and paddy-based agriculture), but in its history (by creating natural boundaries protecting small kingdoms, which in the days when much of northern and eastern India was under control of the Moghul Empire, were allowed to flourish in isolation). They are also significant in her folk religion and culture. [2]

Bengal, from a very early time, has been seen as lying on the fringes of or even beyond the civilization of the upper Gangetic Plains. First, the Vedic Aryans, Brahman orthodoxy, and, later, even the Muslim power centered in Delhi saw the land as dangerous and impure. An investigation into the history of

Bengal reveals features of its social and religious forms that show reactions to these attitudes and serve to place the region even further outside the domination of the Vedic culture and outside the pale of Brahmanic hierarchy. The series of invasions that took place—Pathans (twelfth century), Moghuls (seventeenth century), British (eighteenth century)—not only disrupted socio-economic conditions, but caused cultural, religious, and political changes that enriched Bengali culture. Bengali people, a mixture of the four ethnic groups known to the ethnologists as Kol, Dravidian, Mongolian, and Aryan, [3] learned to accomodate new ideas, and it is no wonder that Bengal became in the nineteenth century the birthplace of a new political and cultural resurgence in India.

Even though there is mention of Bengal in the epic *The Mahāb-hārata* (fourth century B.C.–fourth century A.D.), [4] her history did not begin to be recorded till the eighth century A.D. [5] Jainism and Buddhism from early times had been strong in the eastern part of the subcontinent. These influences might also have been responsible for the restricted entry of Brahmanic orthodoxy and the stunted impact of Aryan civilization in Bengal. A similar anti-orthodox influence continued later (fifteenth–eighteenth centuries) in the somewhat democratic and catholic spirit of Vaishna-vism [6] and other local medieval religious cults such as Tantrism and Sahajiya, [7] which followed the decline of Buddhism in Bengal. The influence of these cults on Bengali literature, religion and philosophy, and social thinking is paramount. In fact, the flexible though emotional quality of these cults laid the foundation of a culture that, throughout its history, discouraged orthodoxy and welcomed new ideas. The same tendency was reflected in the attempt to bring about a synthesis of Hinduism and Islam after the Muslim conquest of Bengal (A.D. 1200), and again in the liberalism and radicalism in response to western ideas that gave rise to the nineteenth-century renaissance after the British takeover of the state.

The mainspring of all these local (*laukik*) cults was the concept of *bhakti* (devotion) that deeply permeated Bengali literature and personality structure. The initial appeal of the *bhakti* movement can be understood by the fact that the established religions such as Vedic Brahmanism and Buddhism had relied upon speculative and metaphysical heights attainable only by the cultured few.

These religions were too abstract, neutral, and impersonal to satisfy the masses. The *bhakti* movement, on the other hand, spared the intellect altogether and offered devotion as the mainstay. It demanded absolute obedience and selfless devotion to a personal god and it increased the hold of religion over a people whose distress in economic, political, and religious life at that time was unparalleled. The Pathan and Moghul rule disrupted the normal Hindu religion and social system. Numerous Bengali legends and folksongs were composed depicting this theme with great despair. The *bhakti* movement had negative aspects as well. Vaishnavism was a great progressive force in its time and produced one of the most lyrical bodies of literature, but it was also responsible for intellectual decline and the emasculation of national life in pre-British Bengal due to its overemotional nature and the almost exclusive attention it paid to the life of love (*prem*) and devotion (*bhakti*) in preference to the life of thought (*jñān*) and action (*karma*). The cult tried to raise the spiritual standard of people without paying attention to social and intellectual levels. Instead of helping its followers to improve the social conditions in which they lived, the cult enticed them away to an unreal world of its own fabrication where Krishna and Rādhā perpetually made love in the flowering groves near the river Yamuna. The effect was intoxicating. For two centuries the *bhaktas* (devotees) sang, danced, and fell into ecstatic trances while the society around them remained both underdeveloped and decadent. *Bhakti* satisfied the craving of the masses for an emotional religion by giving them a god with whom warm and intimate communion could be established as it could between one human being and another. This appeal has very deep roots in the Bengali national tradition of thinking and feeling, and is reflected in literature even today. [8] A good example in modern literature is Tagore, who, despite his strong allegiance to Upanishdic philosophy and western radicalism, could not escape this intoxicating spirit (*mātoārā prān*), as many of his writings reflect. [9] This drug-like effect of emotional abandon and mystical rapture that provides the most insidious escape from the realities of life appears to enter into the personality of Bengali women.

From the religious and cultural point of view, these local cult movements are very significant. Beyond being non-Aryan, and anti-Brahmanic (opposed to the caste system), they brought to focus for the first time a local element (*laukik*)[10] that had been excluded from the classical and aristocratic fold. Not only were some deities brought down to the mass level from their higher abode, but the reverse movement also followed: local gods and goddesses assumed scriptural recognition, and places in the high Hindu pantheon.[11] The aristocracy became initiated into observing these *laukik* rites and transformed *laukik* deities.

Thus, succeeding the Muslim conquest in Bengal, a new folk culture founded on folk religion of a ritualistic nature emerged. The Hindu orthodox Brahmanic clerics (priests-pundits), who had their own culture and economic interests vested in the monopolized use of Sanskrit language and the Sanskritic religion, opposed this, alleging that this folk culture worship of rustic, low-born deities was low, indecent, occult, and lax. But this allegation could not stop the fervor of the mass movement that spread across the state and the eastern part of India, gradually infiltrating the upper class of Hindu society including the Brahmans themselves. An added cause of such infiltration was the economic impoverishment of the Brahmans due to the depletion of sources of livelihood, primarily the patronage of the old royalty and aristocracy. As the *laukik* cults began to be accepted by the high castes, the status of the plebeian deities improved and they began to be accepted by their Olympian relatives. Thus the Sanskritization[12] of the folk religion was achieved. This *laukik* mass movement also brought Hindus and Muslims (mostly converts from lower castes) closer together, perhaps for the first and the last time in Bengal's religious history. The common ground was religious ritual that had relevance to communal living, everyday needs, and aspirations.[13]

By the latter half of the sixteenth century political instability, created by rebellious Hindu sublords against weak Muslim rulers, gave rise to a resurgence of the orthodox Hindu movement under the guidance of neo-Brahmanism. Subsequent social and cultural conflicts reached a climax through increasing antagonism between the Vaishnavism and the Shakta cults of Hinduism, and later in the more serious conflict between the Muslims and the Hindus in the seventeenth and eighteenth centuries.

The groundwork for the Bengali renaissance of the nineteenth century was thus prepared by the constant rebellion against orthodoxy, pedantry, rigidity, and a resurgence of new classicism that was achieved by reinstituting the original sources of Hindu culture. The cultural history of Bengal, including the literature of the nineteenth century, may be regarded as a continuous battle between the conservatism of the Hindu aristocracy and the radicalism of modernism and westernization.

This phase of Bengali culture may also be termed the Calcutta phase [14] because this urban center played an extremely important role in nineteenth-century Bengal. The city of Calcutta owes its origin and supremacy over the whole country of India and its position as the imperial capital of British India entirely to British influence. The rise of Calcutta also marks the swing of the modern Hindu toward European civilization. This modernization and westernization was the result of the impact of British economy, administration, and educational systems. It was also the result of a dissatisfaction accompanying the gradual degeneration of the neo-Hinduism of the earlier conservative Hindu culture.

It was in Bengal that British rule was first firmly established, western education was introduced, and a new economy was set up that led to the birth of a middle-class intelligentsia. This class led the subsequent social, religious, cultural, and political resurgences throughout the nineteenth and twentieth centuries.

The lowest point in the life of Hindu society in Bengal was reached by the end of the eighteenth century when the European contact began. Polygamy and proliferation of ritualism and ostentatious worshipping went hand-in-hand with the utter degradation of women, especially in the institution of *kulinism*. *Kulinism*, an innovation introduced by the orthodox Brahmans, was a device to maintain the purity and rigid boundary of the upper castes through strict endogamy and a rule of commensality. [15] This system led to hypergamy, a high rate of polygamy, and the rites of *sati*, [16] which was still practiced occasionally. Widow-remarriage was totally forbidden among the higher castes. Among men, moral lapses were overlooked. Nirmal Kumar Bose, a prominent social scientist, describes the social condition of Bengal of the time as follows:

It was as if Hindu society tried to hold aloft its banner of purity by relegating that responsibility to the keeping of this noble, but completely misguided, band of heroic women. While the latter burned themselves to death, the rest of society wallowed in abuses and degradation which choked the life of the individual from all directions, unless he secured an escape in religious retirement from the burden and temptations of life. [17]

Decadence, as in most societies, rather than inspiring positive reform or rebellion, led to ill-attempted compromise and grudging acceptance accompanied by cynicism and frustration. This lasted until the challenge of Christian missionary activities finally woke Bengali society from its stupor.

Bengal's contact with the western world during the eighteenth century was crucial. The intellectual impact of the west was first felt by a few Bengali leaders who were attracted by the value of individual freedom. One of them was Raja Rammohon Roy, the foremost of the Bengali reformers, who boldly attacked decadent Hindu society and demanded the abolition of the *sati* and the caste system, the removal of the degradation of women, and the establishment of the right of the individual to live and act according to his or her own judgment. A religious movement led by Rammohon Roy called the Brāhmo Samāj (founded in 1828) tried actively to reform the society. Christian missionary activities were led by foreign missionaries who became personal friends of the suffering peasants and others in backward communities, including the tribes. Their vehement criticism of Hindu religious practices at that time found support from the young intellectuals who became the first organizers and members of the Brāhmo Samāj movement. The leader Rammohon Roy acquired beliefs and values based on the uncompromising monotheism of Islam and the proud rationalism of modern Europe. Influenced by the Christian church, he sought to found a place for people to worship one God. This religious movement in Bengal, which began with a handful of intellectuals looking for an alternative religion shorn of emotionalism, failed to appeal to the masses, but remained a small reform movement instead.

The Brāhmo Samāj movement created a new society of a handful of people working to extract individual freedom from the bondage of caste and religious conservatism. Their pressure succeeded in mobilizing the British government to abolish *sati* in 1829, and to establish legal sanction for widow-remarriage in

1856, even in the face of vehement public opinion against the bill. This movement thus tried to liberate the individual from the authoritarianism of a rigid social order, supporting the rights of the individual in social life as it existed rather than the idea of renunciation (bairāgya), the total subordination of the individual to authority and tradition.

Journals were founded as the mouthpiece of the movement now primarily based on social reform, education, and humanitarian services. Progressive young men believing in this movement also became keenly interested in the education and emancipation of women. A journal was published for women and schools were established for girls; the movement spread not only across the state but to other parts of India as well. A new turn of the movement was taken by introducing the element of bhakti in order to counteract and counterbalance the emphasis on rational knowledge (jñān). Men and women became equal in praying to God. The Native Marriage Act in 1872 legalized unorthodox cross-caste marriage, made monogamy obligatory, and fixed the minimum age for the bridegroom at eighteen and for the bride at fourteen. The attempt of this phase of the Brāhmo Samāj movement to achieve a synthesis between western rationalism and medieval Hindu devotion kept the movement alive for a while, but this soon subsided and was followed by a resurgence of neo-Hinduism led by Vivekananda and Ramkrishna. The schism in the Brāhmo Samāj between the rational and the bhakti groups helped the revival of Hinduism in Bengal and elsewhere, movements such as Ārya Samāj in the north, and the Theosophic Society in south India.

The same attempt to synthesize rationalism and devotion was attempted again in neo-Hinduism. The main objective was to revive the Purānic[18] religion of the middle era and establish ritualistic orthodox customs in everyday life. Writers such as Bankim Chandra Chatterjee tried to infuse new life into moribund Hinduism along with westernized ideas of romanticism borrowed from the west and bhakti borrowed from the medieval cults. Bankim claimed that knowledge (jñān) and action (karma) ideally lead to bhakti. Some authors even tried to explain Purānic religion and culture by means of European logic and philosophy; for example, Krishna was reinterpreted for his humanitarianism.

Along with the theistic reform movement of the Brāhmo Samāj there were parallel movements in the field of education that opened doors toward agnosticism or atheism; in short, movements towards a secularization of reform. The establishment of the Hindu College (Presidency College) in 1817 in Calcutta made English education available to Indians and became the center for new ideas and youth movements such as the Young Bengal movement, one of the most invigorating and controversial phases of Bengal renaissance. [19] This group of talented youth believed in freedom, truth, the supreme value of justice and patriotism, philanthropy, and self-abnegation.

This three-way flow of the theistic reform movement of Brāhmo Samāj, restoration of orthodox Hinduism, and the secularization of freedom generated by English education and the new economy can be said to have produced what modern Bengal is today. The society and culture as reflected in people's lives have become an interesting mixture of ideas and symbols representing all three kinds of movements. Interesting consequences may be noticed in the division of different ideals followed by different strata of the society. For example, the middle-class intelligentsia within the direct professional rubric of modern economy were urbanized and were more secularized than the landed gentry. The life of the latter still drew on a rural-based economy, and until recently protected the interests of the upper castes (kulin), continuing orthodox Hinduism. Some continued to live a dual life compartmentalized on one hand by western secularism and on the other by the rituals and customs of conservative Hinduism. In this section of society the dichotomy in some cases is reflected in the attitude and life style of men who represent secular western values and in the life style of women who stress conservative Hindu values. In this there is some influence from male to female.

With the economy becoming more market-oriented and the British-built railways connecting smaller towns to bigger cities, selective migration to the towns began. The rich left the villages for education or professional opportunities and became interested in improving the medical, educational, and other facilities in the town, giving rise to a new economic class of factory owners, traders, schoolteachers, medical men. All these professional men came from a limited number of originally prosperous castes that had taken advantage of education or had the means to migrate. Another striking fact was that while the new economic class was interested in the west they continued to invest in cash (secured from trade or a profession) in landed property because the investment in land appeared safe under the existing insecure political conditions. This newly emerged, newly urbanized, economically wealthy upper caste turned into landlords and began to spend a large proportion of their wealth in building temples, big houses, and in conspicuous expenditure during religious or social festivals as status symbols of ostentatious living.

Women

These changes in the economy and the professions of men have not altered the life pattern of men and women inside families. Women have remained more or less secluded within the inner house, segregated from the men's world of the outer house. The courtyard surrounded by rooms and the roof terrace are still the places where women retire in the afternoon for fresh air and to gossip. Like the ornamental elements of European design that began to appear in some wealthy homes, western influence has remained superficial.

These upper-class and upper middle-class families are products of the historical, cultural, and social movements mentioned before. These are the families whose fathers and forefathers had landed properties in rural Bengal but mostly moved to Calcutta and vicinity during the last two generations. Some produced prominent leaders in the Brāhmo Samāj or the Hindu revival movements. Their women, while going to school and being exposed to western as well as Indian educational systems, are not completely encouraged to live an independent life based on a profession, except in a few extraordinary cases where such is practiced to demonstrate an ideal about the status of women. School and college education for the women are encouraged as a status symbol, and this helps in marriage negotiations. Moreover, such education is not expected to change the ideas and thoughts of a woman and make her disregard the traditional values based on both conservative Hinduism and ritualistic folk customs that are a part of everyday living. The classical idea of a woman being the custodian of family religion and solidarity persists very strongly. It is interesting that despite the Brāhmo Samāj and Radical Hindu and missionary movements, all of which empha- sized education for women, the practice and meaning of education for women came to be of a restricted kind in this class. Reasons may be found partly in the lack of the economic necessity of pushing women into jobs (thereby reducing the seriousness of vocational education). Perhaps more important, the conserva- tism of the Brahmanical *kulin* culture dominated by men still lingers, despite the fact that some women do go out to work in the world outside their households.

Women of this class are released from engrossing physical labor within the family because the families can easily afford hired help for household work. Consequently, the women have enough leisure to chat, read, listen to radio programs, go to movies, or brood.

A word must be added here regarding the role literary sources and mass media (movies, radio, stage performances, the per- forming arts of both a religious and secular kind) play in reinforcing certain expectations in a Bengali woman's life. How this happens is discussed in the chapter on childhood and adolescence. Let me briefly touch on the subject here by stating that a particular kind of literary source and mass media with strong emphasis on romantic love seem to play a very significant role in an upper-class woman's socialization process. Moreover, similar types of literary sources continue to feed her romantic imagination and needs, even after she is married. A woman's romantic expectations, intensified by the romantic ideals Bengali literature and mass media emphasize, have little connection with real life. Literature or any other form of creative art, although it reflects reality, also exaggerates it and often exaggerates only those aspects of life that are beautiful and unattainable. Many thrive on reading such literature, which makes them aware of feelings they may not be able to articulate. This is especially true in the case of romantic novels and poetry. Sociological data of nineteenth-century Europe and classical India (A.D. 400) support this; the magnificent romantic literature in these times and places triggered off traditions of romantic love based on ideals and myth rather than reality. A young Bengali girl recognizes her partially formed feelings of romantic love when she reads Vaishnava poetry,[20] for instance, where exquisite lyrics express Rādhā's ecstatic love, or when she reads Shakespeare's verses on Romeo's dream and desire for his beloved, or when she watches a love story on the movie screen.

Because of the sociocultural background of the type of Bengali women we are concerned with here, western literature, mass media, and sports become very significant as socializing and enculturating agents. Her romantic imagination during adolescence is influenced a great deal by the western romantic tradition as well. At the same time, she is also exposed to very selective pieces from the romantic literature of classical and modern India; the result is a unique mixture that enhances her expectations and aspirations.

Marriage and Household Composition

The group of families I call the upper class and upper middle-class, semi-urbanized and urbanized Bengalis (henceforward called upper class), practice caste endogamy and *gotra* exogamy. *Gotra* is an exogamous category within a caste whose principal use is to regulate marriage matches. All members of a *gotra* are presumed to be descended from or associated with the same supernatural source. People of different castes may carry the same *gotra* name and claim descent from the same legendary sage or deity.[21]

Sociocultural and economic backgrounds of families are considered very important in marriage negotiations. Families of the bride and groom are expected to be of about the same social status. Equality is sought in wealth, in education (men and women having higher university degrees especially from foreign universities), and general reputation (what neighbors, distant relatives and servants think about the families). Once such matters are satisfactorally established, the bridegroom's education, job, conduct, and personal appearance are considered. As for the bride, personal appearance, education, conduct and manners, reputation in housework, needlework, and so on, are of importance. All these conditions are to some extent negotiable. Marriages, almost without exception, are arranged by families often with the help of a matchmaker, relative, servant, or friend.

While equality in reputation and wealth of the two families is sought, a lavish dowry of cash and gifts may be offered by the bride's family to make a match in a family of higher status, especially if the bridegroom is endowed with higher earning potential. A family's status and reputation are tested whenever a wedding takes place. The more money spent, the larger the number of guests and the more gifts offered, the more prestigious the marriage appears to outsiders. Weddings of this class involve great expenditure, much gift-giving, and large attendance by kin, friends, and neighbors of the two families.

Families are patrilineal in descent and patrilocal in residence. When a bride joins her husband's family she becomes a member of his lineage for most purposes—ritual, economic, and legal. But she also retains some affiliation with her original lineage and some rights in it. For example, she can always go back to her natal family or to her father's relatives. The joint-family remains the most important group an individual belongs to and toward which he has rights and duties prescribed. A joint-family is fraternal, with the father and the older brothers as the *de jure* heads and the mother and the older daughters-in-law as the *de jure* heads in the realm of food consumption, distribution, childrearing. The ideal of filial-fraternal solidarity is very highly stressed. This ideal demands that brothers and their family units should live together in the same household, sharing equally in one economic fund, in common property, and contributing to the family to their best ability. The joint ownership of property is assumed by law and implies joint living. One or two brothers may live separately in other cities because of professional opportunities. But this is by necessity rather than by choice. The first and foremost duty of a male member is to contribute to the family fund, no matter where he is, and gather together with the other members on such occasions as weddings, funerals, Puja festivals,[22] and so on. Women who come to the joint-family as wives must also uphold the ideal of this filial-fraternal solidarity.

The joint-family economy may depend on several sources. If it is a family that migrated to the city for educational and professional facilities, there still may remain some landed property in the village and the revenue may be realized through employed assistants. However, the major part of the income comes from the salaried professions of the male members. The professions commonly practiced are medicine, law, college professorships, or responsible administrative positions in the government. A woman has the right to be supported by her husband's joint-family until her death. If her sons split up after the death of the father (for such various reasons as conflict or jobs in other places), as a widow she is sure to be supported by one of her sons. If she is unfortunate enough not to have a son, she may be taken care of by one of her classificatory nephews or, under very special circumstances, by her daughter and the daughter's family. She may also go back to her natal family and live with one of her brothers. These alternatives are taken only if she does not have a son to look after her in her old age.

Family Roles

A few words on family roles need mentioning at this point. Major roles ascribed by birth (son, daughter, father, mother, siblings, grandparents) and achieved by marriage (husband, wife, father-in-law, brothers-in-law, sisters-in-law, mother-in-law) become of special interest in the Bengali case because of the joint living situation and because of very well-defined role-ideals and normative behavior. Every person occupying a role-set within his joint-family knows exactly what is expected of him and what he can expect in a dyadic or multiple role-interaction. These normative behaviors stressed by an ideal founded in traditional familial values are stereotypes of proper family behavior and serve as guides to its members. In reality, the tensions and irregularities may not always be successfully ironed out by rules that are nothing but broad outlines within which variations of behavior occur, as will be shown throughout the following pages.

2 Childhood and Adolescence

Birth and Early Months

Unlike rural and lower-class families, upper-class and upper middle-class families do not consider a girl's birth to be a sad affair.[1] If she happens to be the firstborn the family rejoices at her birth in the same way they rejoice at the arrival of a male child. Apart from a few cryptic remarks on the part of a grandmother, nothing negative is said. The grandmother may comment on her complexion and her physical appearance and speculate on the potential value of the girl as a bride. She may also warn the mother and the father that they should start saving cash for the big dowry that may be necessary for a good catch for such an unpromising thing. All these are said and listened to half-jokingly. However, from the very first day of her birth the fact that she is born to be married and to bring honor and peace to her family is clear in everybody's mind and is heightened off and on through such comments.

She is cared for and caressed with great affection and tenderness by all the women in the family. Men do not come in close contact with her until she is three or four years old. There may be a maid hired especially to take care of her physical needs: bathing, washing her diapers, massaging her with mustard oil before her bath, and so on. However, most of this is basically the mother's, grandmother's, and other women's jobs. Among the other women, the wives of the father's brothers, the widowed sister (if any) of the father, and the father's unmarried sisters are most important. The daughters of the father's brothers, if they are old enough, may also take a great deal of interest in looking after the new baby. A great deal of time is spent on the baby by all the women of the joint household. When she is not being carried, she either sleeps in a swinging crib or, if it is winter, she may spend the early morning playing in the sun on the roof. At night she sleeps with her mother. This may last at least until the time of weaning, some time in the second or third year. (The same bed may be shared by the father and one or two other siblings, but the baby is always next to the mother.) The time of weaning may be hastened by the arrival of another sibling. [2]

At this age she is handled, cared for, carried, dressed, massaged, and decorated with eye-ointment after her bath in exactly the same way as her male counterpart. There is hardly any difference in treatment until weaning. At that time, however, treatment may be markedly different, particularly if she has a male sibling. Immediately, most of her care will be transferred to one of the father's brothers' wives or to the maid, or perhaps to both.

Early Childhood

When she begins to walk, most of her time will be spent with other girls in the house, perhaps her paternal cousins. Boys and girls play together until the boys reach six or seven. The games usually consist of imitating the household they live in. The boys pretend to be the men in the family, and the girls divide among themselves the roles of mother-in-law and sisters-in-law. I have noticed little girls pulling their skirts over their heads as if they were using the end of a sari as younger married women do in the presence of older affines. They also imitate terms of address when they talk to each other: *kartā*, which is used both to address and to refer to the oldest male member in the household by his wife, is often used by the girls while playing old ladies. They will use terms for each other such as *baro bau* (the oldest wife, i.e., the oldest sister-in-law) or *mejo bau* (the middle sister-in-law). It is interesting to note the nuances of emotional content in the relationships that they pick up from their observations even at this early age (three to five). One sister-in-law may be found to complain to her mother-in-law against another when she is not around as they play these roles.

This is also the age when the young girl is around the women of the house a great deal watching them cooking, chatting, gossiping, or engaging in religious activities. She may often find it amusing to watch the maid clean the *thākur ghar* (the household shrine) where so many intriguing pictures and effigies stand. She watches her grandmother or one of her older aunts performing the daily rites of offering the deities food and flowers and she listens to the chants (*pānchāli* and *brata kathā*),[3] which fascinate her. While watching this, she keeps asking questions as to who is supposed to be what god and whether they really come to accept the offerings. The answers to such queries are usually vague. She is attracted by the whole game with dolls and pictures, so like that which she and her sisters and cousins play. She may also accompany her grandmother to religious meetings or temples in the early evening, where many women of grand-mother's age gather to listen to recitations from the holy books, *The Rāmāyana* and *The Mahābhārata*. The grandmother may also visit the temple for a short while to meditate or see her guru (see chap. 4), while the little girl watches others or goes browsing through the toys and sweets in shops nearby. From these visits she learns to respect the temple, feeling drawn by the smell of flowers, sandalwood, and incense. In her later life the combina-tion of such aromas may, on many occasions, evoke the memory of a religious setting (see chap. 4).

Around the age of five or six, the girl is also supposed to begin her studies along with her other siblings (both her own and classificatory). The very first year or two may be the responsi-bility of the mother or a younger aunt, or perhaps an older sister, who introduces her to the alphabet, both Bengali and English. In some households a private tutor may be employed to teach all the children their first lessons in the alphabet and numbers. Here the girl is treated equally with her male siblings. She may also be admitted to a primary school after a couple of years of home tutoring. The age at which she goes to school may vary between six and ten, depending on the way the family feels about it. Her mother may want to coach her longer on her own before giving her to a school. This, however, depends on how free the mother is before the next child arrives and also on her ability and desire to tutor her daughter. Other members of the family may feel that she is not yet ready to face a school atmosphere.

When she begins to attend school, the responsibility of looking after her education shifts to one of the male members of the family. It usually falls to the father or an uncle, or even the grandfather (if he is not too old), whoever has spare time in the evenings. This, in fact, is the beginning of a stage when the daughter encounters and spends considerable time with her father or a father figure. Before this age her only contact with her father is perhaps an occasional encounter when he may pick her up and give a light kiss on the cheek; or he may bring occasional gifts to her. But this is unlikely if she happens to be one of the many classificatory siblings of her age. She may on her own come running to him to complain about another sibling or a servant, but she never spends time either talking or sitting with him. When she begins to go to school, she spends two or three hours in the evening with her father, doing her homework. These sessions include more than teaching and learning. During them, she learns how to play upon her father's emotions and how to manipulate the situation when he is harsh with her if she cannot spell a word or fails to do a sum. She may weep over a small rebuke and throw a tantrum until the father is embarrassed into reconciliation. She usually wins. Many of these sessions may end up with the father apologizing and making up for his strict criticism. He takes her on his lap, wipes her tears, and caresses her until she smiles again and runs off to have her dinner. She may even summon her mother's help if the situation gets beyond her control.

During these sessions, the grandmother may come by to supervise what goes on. She comments on the fact that it is stupid to make girls go through such hard work; after all, what they will be doing is looking after a husband and son. ⁴She does not see any reason why her little granddaughter has to go through these difficult books in order to make a good wife and a good mother. Has she, herself, made a bad mother because she never went to school or her father never spent evenings teaching her how to multiply? With this the grandmother may even try to snatch the girl away by saying that she will be better off listening to the old lady or watching what is going on in the kitchen. The father tolerates such intrusions with studied indifference. If he happens to be a favorite son of his mother, he may attempt a mild argument, saying that his mother would have lost nothing if her father had taught her how to multiply. In fact, as a child he would have liked the idea of his mother teaching him a few elementary things. The tone of these arguments is never serious. The crux of the grandmother's position is a warning to her son against going too far over a girl's education. The same scene may be repeated time and again as the father sits with the daughter for evening tutoring. The mother of the girl, on the other hand, does not object to her learning to read and write; in fact, she herself has been the first tutor for the girl. She only objects to her spending too much time on her schoolwork with her father. The mother feels it may not be a good idea to let her daughter be influenced by her husband in all sorts of bookish ideas that are not helpful in learning about real life. The mother's argument is as follows: Her husband has little knowledge (according to her) about the world in which women move. He does not, for example, understand all her frustrations at being in a joint household with five other women from five different families. As he has little sympathy for his own wife's plight, what can he teach his daughter that will be good for her future? Therefore, the daughter is unlikely to gain anything by spending hours with him. After all, he does not intend to make a lawyer or a civil servant out of this daughter of his! Besides, no matter what he plans for her, her destiny is to spend her life in her *sasur-bāri*.[5] She will have to go through the same roles of mother, daughter-in-law, and sister-in-law as her mother did. *Her* father sent her to school, and *she* was a good student. What good has come of it? What she learned from books does not help her today in coping with her family problems. Her father also wanted her to go to college; but her grandmother was dead against it. Looking back, she thanks her grandmother for this, even though she resented it at the time. What would she have gained with a college degree?

While this remains the mother's rationale for not encouraging the daughter to spend too much time with her father, she suffers from a tinge of jealousy. In a joint household, where the wife rarely sees the husband alone outside the bedroom at night, her daughter is one of the women who is allowed to spend a great deal of time with him. It is quite acceptable. The father, who is apparently helping the daughter only with her schoolwork, is also enjoying talking to her and playing little emotional games, teasing her and being teased in return, or scolding her and making up for it later. He is very close to this little woman who entertains him and who is going to go away some day very soon to become the daughter of another man. The relationship, from the very beginning, is charged with this imminent pain of separation that every father must go through. This knowledge on the part of both the father and the daughter seems to make the naturally close relationship even more intense. Second, the fact that the women in the house are continuously trying to interfere with this close bond indirectly reinforces it. A very deep bond develops between them, as it were, and against the women's world. During the daughter's early age, it remains a close bond of affection; later it becomes one of companionship and friendship. For the daughter at this stage, the father is an emotional ally, even though he may be strict and critical about her schoolwork. She accepts the harshness with grace because her love and confidence in him also encourage her to pay a lot of attention to what he says.

Other Men in the Household

Even as early as six or seven, the young girl sees the importance of the men's world for her retreat from the world of women. She notices, for example, if her mother scolds her over something, one of the uncles may come by and compensate for it by giving her a sweet or promising a trip to the zoo. He may even mildy scold the mother for being so harsh with the little thing. She may be addressed "mother" by her uncles or even her father. They treat her with great interest and affection, particularly if she happens to be the firstborn in the joint household.

Case no. 1: My father's mother died about fifteen months before I was born. All my uncles thought grandmother was reincarnated in me. They all called me "mother" and often compared parts of my body with those of grandmother's. I knew, for example, my feet were exactly like hers, equally graceful and pretty. This went on to the extent that my grandfather, who still missed his wife, constantly teased me that soon he was going to marry me because I was the obvious replacement. I recall my anger at this suggestion of marrying such an old man, even though I was very fond of grandfather. Since my uncles and father called me "mother" and treated me as their lost mother, I felt great affection toward them. I would often be asked by the neighbors how many sons I had. I would answer them with pride—five. This used to be a very common theme of conversation whenever the neighbors saw me.

Case no. 2: Even at the age of five I could sense that my uncles (and one in particular) were very fond of me. Every afternoon each would bring some gift or other. They all had different terms to call me. I was the "little flower" to my youngest uncle, my father's younger brother; "the fair one" to my uncle older than my father, and "the mother" to the oldest one. My father, of course, always called me "my little mother," I guess, to avoid confusion between his real mother and me. I also knew which one of my uncles would be most useful in particular adverse situations. If my mother wanted to punish me because I broke a toy or a glass or stole a sweetmeat from the kitchen, I always approached my older uncles who would scold mother for being so harsh. Because mother was not supposed to answer them back, she had to swallow such reprimand without protest. If I really did something terribly wrong, such as beating up my younger brother, then, of course, my mother or grandmother would beat me up, too. In those situations I would go to my youngest uncle in his study and weep in his lap without bothering to tell him what happened. He never asked, I guess, because he could tell that I was at fault. I liked my youngest uncle most because I could always go to him and weep without being questioned. He usually smiled and changed the subject by telling me a story or reading from his book. He also took me to places and brought me the most beautiful dolls. At times, my mother would be annoyed with him and scold him mildly for spoiling me. She often lamented the fact that it was impossible to discipline me or train me for anything while all the men in the family were determined to spoil me. To that my uncle would smile and ask my mother, "But, *boudi* [older sister-in-law], weren't you also spoiled the same way when you were a little girl?" Mother would utter an emphatic "No, never."

If the girl's father is busy most of the time, his older brothers may have more time for her—even more so if the older brothers have no daughters and she happens to be particularly good looking and pleasing in temperament. They provide her with attention and affection, not so much in talking and spending time with her, but in giving her things—toys, sweets. A particular uncle may like her to sleep in his room, which is considered a great gesture of closeness. In fact, the cousins may fight with each other over the right to sleep with one uncle or the other.

Case no. 3: I hardly ever slept with my parents after I was four. I rotated almost every night between my various uncles and sometimes my grandmother. But it was difficult to have any space in her bed because all the grandsons slept in her bed. It was no fun sleeping away from her next to one of those boys who kicked me all night. So I preferred to sleep in *baro-jyathā's* [father's older brother] bed, who was very nice and put his arms around me in winter. However, I missed the nice stories grandmother told my cousins. Later, when I was ten or twelve I often shared the same bed with my female cousins, and we would chat in bed till one of our mothers would order us to hush up and go to sleep. I do not quite remember the conversations. Mostly we talked about our dolls and their weddings.

The relationship between her and her grandfather is one of constant teasing and joking. He plays the role of an old seducer. He never inquires about her schoolwork; he may save a candy or fruit to give her when the others (usually his grandsons) are not around. This is also his way of bribing her to spend an afternoon with him, pulling out his gray hairs when he dozes off for his midday nap. Pulling out gray hair is also part of the responsibility that a granddaughter has toward her grandmother. But it is much more fun to pull the grandfather's hair because the renumeration is usually higher. Besides, the sweets and candies and the teasing and joking that go with it are also more attractive than fingering through grandmother's greasy long hair and listening to her dry advice.

Case no. 4: Consider the following conversation between an eight-year-old girl and her seventy-year-old grandfather:

Grandfather: I see my little wife is very busy. How about stopping for a minute here and sit down next to me. I have something to give you.

Granddaughter: Stop that. Didn't I tell you thousands of times not to call me your little wife? I am not your wife and never shall be. Your wife is the old lady who is chanting the names of all the gods in Heaven. I shall never marry anyone, let alone an old man like you.

Grandfather: But don't you know all granddaughters are the wives of their grandfathers? Oh, I know you wish to marry your other grandfather, your mother's father. Is that what it is? But, look, that old man is very stingy, I hear. He will never give you saris and jewelry.

Granddaughter: Who cares! I am not interested in either of you. Now forget the marriage. What do you have to give me? Quick, I am getting late.

Grandfather: Come close. I have saved something for you. But first, promise, you will come back after lunch to give a head-massage.

Granddaughter: Oh, a *sandesh* [a sweetmeat]! How nice. Yes, yes, I shall come back later, but you will have to tell me more stories.

The grandfather also enjoys talking to the granddaughter about, perhaps, his dead wife, his youth, his childhood, his mother. No other person in the house has that much time and attention to give him. His relationship with his own sons and daughters-in-law is somewhat distant and formal for such conversations. Among the grandchildren, the boys have no patience to sit and listen. It also appears as if he himself has less patience with his grandsons than with his granddaughters. At this age (seventy to eighty), he often becomes talkative and as naïve as a child. He feels free to tell her all that he likes to recall. He finds a listener; she finds his stories as fascinating as fairy tales, more interesting perhaps because she knows some of the heroes and heroines. She learns what her father was like when he was a boy, how her mother looked when she was brought to this household as a new bride, and what a stormy night it was when she was born. These events that took place in the family before she was born fascinate her. She keeps them as secret treasures, perhaps to be told to her own grandchildren someday. This stimulates her imagination, and she begins to make connections between life and the books she reads.

Case no. 5: My grandmother was very good at telling us stories, mostly folktales. In the evening all of my cousins and brothers and sisters would wait for her to come to bed to tell us at least one story before we fell asleep. Some evenings it was hard to keep awake, because she would supervise everybody's dinner before coming to us. Of all the stories she told us, I loved the one with the king and his three queens most, and I begged her to tell the same one repeatedly. My brother, on the other hand, liked ghost stories. I did not care for them because they were too scary, but he liked them precisely because they were so scary. Anyway, I loved to listen to the story of the three queens because I felt very sad for the third queen who was not loved by the king at all. Every time I heard that story, I wept and often dreamed of her as if I was in the same kingdom. My grandfather, on the other hand, told me things from his childhood. How big his house was and how many horses they had. I loved to hear one particular episode when the dacoits came one night to take the money and jewelry away. They came with big torches and guns and killed a servant who was very faithful and tried to save my grandfather's old uncle's life. Listening to those stories, I tried to imagine the women in the big house shivering in fear and screaming. Even though these stories were scary, too, I did not mind listening to them. Later, much later, when I began to read Bankim Chandra's novels in my high school days, I could enjoy them because his characters seemed like the people grandfather talked about.

Thus, while the father is the most significant among the men she is dealing with, her contact with him is less frequent and perhaps less close than in her relationship with her grandfather, uncles, and older male siblings. But her father remains her "hero" and "guru" (teacher). Her father is also the man who has some kind of close relation with her mother, and that is not quite clear to her. She senses a tension between herself and her mother if she becomes too close to her father. She often hears her mother accusing her father of spoiling her, in answer to which the father usually smiles. If the girl happens to know anything about the sexual relationship between the mother and father, she is ambivalent about it, but that does not tarnish her love and respect for her father. If she has already learned about the facts of life from her peers (such as that parents have intercourse), she may also know that sex is considered dirty because no one is supposed to talk about it or watch it. Only adult married people can indulge in it in privacy. And if her parents indulge in it, she is puzzled and may blame her mother for it.

Case no. 6: I adored my father and wanted to marry someone like him. I even told my friends that. I was six at that time when one night I woke up in the middle of the night and found my parents very close together in the bed my father and I shared. Mother was whispering and while they were talking, I could feel something was going on. I disliked being in the same bed with them. First I thought I would indicate that I was up, but decided against it and tried to listen to what they were talking about. I could not make it out. It was clear, however, that both were very excited. I lay there like a stone and tried to go back to sleep; I could not. Next morning I could not look at my father and I hated my mother. It took me quite a few days to get over this. I learned from my friends at school that this happens to all parents.

This knowledge of something exclusive between the mother and father that she does not share along with her love and adoration for her father combine to create an attraction that is strong and ambivalent. She knows he is unattainable, but adorable and attractive. Her father never jokes with her as the grandfather does; perhaps that is why she does not quite adore and admire the grandfather the way she does her father. She is less tense with her father's brothers, but the father has more attraction for her.

Case no. 7: I remember one incident. Father was gone for a few days on a trip. I could see mother was worried about him; perhaps she felt lonely. She often asked me if grandfather said anything about any letter from father. She would ask me and my brothers if we thought father was going to come that day. I understood her feelings well because I missed father very much. This was also the first time I could sympathize with my mother. I almost felt I was her companion rather than the competitor this time.

Case no. 8: One thing I was never clear about was the relationship between my parents. I knew very early that they have something special between them that no other people in the household did, but I could not quite grasp it. Once I recall I asked my father what mother was to him. He replied, "She is my wife and your mother." That's all. I was six at that time. I heard from my older sister later that when I was younger I would refer to all my aunts as the mothers of their husbands. At that time the only relationship that existed for me was that between a mother and a child. But as I grew older it did not make sense. Then I learned from my friends at school that all parents have sexual relations because they are married. Then my trouble was to find out if absolutely all married people did such bad things. Even though I watched my parents once in a while, I could never tell if grandfather and grandmother, for example, ever did it. They were married, too. I was convinced they did not, and that's why I liked them better, I thought. Since my parents hardly spent time together joking or laughing as did my grandparents or my mother and *choto kākā* [father's younger brother], I concluded that only those people who are not too friendly had sex. I was rather pleased that my parents had it, even though I disliked the idea terribly. I could console myself because my father would never be friendly with my mother. He loved me more than he loved her. Although I always wanted to marry someone like my father, there were times when I preferred to marry my young uncle. I did not want to have a husband who would be like the husband my father was to my mother. All this made me feel rather sorry for my mother at times, although usually I did not like her.

Mother and Mother-Figures

During this time the girl also watches her mother playing the role of a good wife, good daughter-in-law, and good mother, though she is not sure about the first two. She cannot quite tell what being a good wife means. If her mother is the wife of her father, then, except occasionally in bed (and still she is not sure), they hardly spend any time together. Whenever they meet the mother usually complains about the children, the servants, or other members of the household, while the father gives lip-service to such complaints by remaining quiet or by taking sides with the mother in a diplomatic fashion. He makes it clear that he will not take any steps to solve the problem. If the complaint happens to be against one of his brothers' wives, to whom he was particularly close before his marriage (see the section on brother-in-law/sister-in-law in chap. 3), he treats the matter with diplomacy.

All this the daughter may overhear or encounter. She begins to sense the factions within the household.

Case no. 9: One night I woke up on hearing some loud conversation. My mother was sobbing and talking at the same time. She sounded very distressed, and father was just repeating, "Quiet, quiet. They will hear; for heaven's sake, lower your voice." I did not know at that time by "they" he meant the others in the family. I was very unhappy to watch my mother weep and tried to understand why. It seemed as if mother felt misunderstood and badly treated by my oldest aunt, who came from a very wealthy family. According to mother's interpretation this aunt did not like her because mother did not come from a similarly wealthy background. Mother also complained bitterly because my father always took sides with this aunt. To that father said, "You women are always jealous of one another. I don't see any unjust behavior. Besides, *boudi* [older sister-in-law] has always been kind to me, and it was she who selected you as my wife, remember? So you do not like the idea that she is like a mother to me. Don't forget when she came to this house as a new bride, I was only fourteen, and she replaced my dead mother. I don't see why you complain. Is not Dipu [father's younger brother] close to you? It's the same thing. Wait till Dipu gets married, you would do the same with his wife." To this my mother sobbed even harder and said, "You always take her side."

She watches her mother do housework with apparently great responsibility and sometimes pleasure. For example, the wife may enjoy preparing a particular dish of fish or dessert that her husband likes. The women of the house, however, do not spend a lot of time in the kitchen except occasionally to prepare a particular delicacy that one of the male members of the family likes. The girl notices the jealousy that the other women feel when her mother's cooking is openly praised by the grandfather or one of the uncles. (Father never makes any comments on mother's cooking, because in a joint household, a man is considered shameless if he openly appreciates his own wife and children. He *must* pretend not to notice.)

She watches her mother and her aunts enjoying the long summer afternoons when they relax with other women or by themselves. These younger women (her aunts and older sisters) recline on beds, chew betel-leaf and nut, [6] gossip, listen to radio programs, and browse through popular journals. The daughter, however, is not allowed to be there, because they are having "adult talk," as her mother puts it. This is the time when the daughter may be called for small services, such as bringing a glass of water for the lady who nearly chokes on betel-nut while giggling, or seeing if the servants have finished their lunch, or she may go up on the roof to see if the pickles are drying properly or if the crows are getting to them. In other words, she receives orders from the mother, or one of the aunts, to do odd jobs if she shows herself in the area. If she is not so curious about "adult talk" she may avoid all this by being away in her grandfather's room listening to his stories while pulling out his gray hair or giving him a leg massage. But she is very curious about these afternoon sessions that her mother and other women have, and she is not quite sure what goes on there. She wonders if she will have the same leisure, with lots of giggling and apparent fun, when she is married.

The younger women in the house may also spend the afternoon listening to the special radio programs designed for housewives, or go to a matinee. She may beg to be taken along, and occasionally an aunt may take her with them. For these outings the women spend hours dressing up. They help with each other's hair and discuss the selection of saris to wear. She enjoys listening to such discussions and watching them dress. She may even participate by passing a comment or two as to which particular sari will look nice. One of her aunts may even ask her opinion on the selection of a particular piece of jewelry. She watches all this with great attention, beginning with how they groom their hair and ending with how they finally get ready with the last draping of the sari along the curves of their bodies. She feels almost envious of their bodies, with round breasts and hips and long, glossy hair. She wonders how long she must wait before she can acquire all these physical endowments. She learns to appreciate the particular kind of physical beauty that is desirable among women. From the conversations among the women, she can tell that she must be presentable in order to attract a good match. She will have to learn now to preserve her long hair and good looks until the time comes for her marriage.

Case no. 10: Every afternoon my mother, no matter how busy she was, would call me to braid my hair. I tried to avoid this because she always pulled my hair too hard and ran the sharp teeth of the comb too deep, hurting me. I screamed and she would repeat the same words everytime: "Don't you want to have nice long hair like *kākimā* [wife of uncle]? No one would like to choose you for a daughter-in-law if you do not have long hair. You must take care of it this way." From this I was nearly convinced that hair of women grew so long because they pulled it so hard. She also gave a similar rationale for my taking regular baths in winter and keeping my fingernails clean and clipped. She also told me repeatedly that I must not walk like a horse or a boy, because these things are very important. No one will choose me for a daughter-in-law if I do not have manners. Sometimes, a woman from the neighborhood would come to chat in the afternoon, and I would be summoned to give her a cup of tea or a glass of water. The woman would give a keen look at me and comment, "Oh, mother of . . ., you are lucky. Your daughter has beautiful eyes. She is also so obedient and gentle. Mine is so bad-tempered and she is also growing like a horse, no gentleness about her at all. I do not know what will happen to her." Then I overheard my grown sisters and cousins talk over their toiletting sessions. They would discuss the way they looked, and one would tease the other. "Come, come, move from the mirror and let me have a look. You are quite pretty already. Why bother to increase it. All the young men in the *pārā* [neighborhood] would go crazy if you looked better."

She also notices that after marriage it becomes unimportant to preserve these endowments. These messages are given to her indirectly through instructions that the married women give teenagers during toiletting sessions. The instructions will be more direct if the group happens to be getting ready to go to a wedding. Her older female siblings will be especially encouraged to dress so that some guests in the wedding may be attracted enough to pursue a possible negotiation for a match. A neighbor's or relative's wedding is a place for such openings (see chap. 3).

Such consciousness about physical endowments, which are important to enhance a better marriage-match, is often reflected in the games the young girl plays at this stage. By now she is between eight and ten. Most of her playmates are girls of similar age who are her siblings and neighbors. They imitate the way women talk, chew their betel-leaf and nuts, and go out to movies or on shopping sprees. She may manage to pick up a few toiletting ingredients from a cousin's dressing-table and betel-leaves from an aunt's bowl. She uses a handkerchief or a towel over her head to indicate long hair and may put some stuffing under her dress to pretend she has breasts. She also has dolls to play with. The roles that are chosen in these games consist mostly of those of the younger women in the household. The aspects of their youth and beauty are emphasized more than their roles as daughters-in-law or wives. In these games, the mother-in-law is absent and so are the male members of the family.

Adolescence

Her contact with her grandmother and older aunts brings another element to her upbringing. Some afternoons after lunch she may be summoned by one of the older aunts to read parts of holy books such as *The Rāmāyana* and *The Mahābhārata* or *The Purānas*,[7] because the aunt cannot quite see the small print or cannot read because she never learned how. These women know the holy books by heart, and during these long summer afternoons when the younger women are amusing themselves with gossip the older women like to listen to parts of the great stories of Sitā, Sāvitri, and Behulā. Apart from amusing themselves, they also feel it is important for the little girl to know about this so that she will remember the great virtuous women of the epics. The little girl should be made conscious of the tradition of the pious, tolerant, and sacrificing women of her country. She should learn the virtue of being like them, so they pick the chapters in which such women loom large, and which they like to listen to time and again. These stories, which the girl knows nearly by heart by the time she is ten, mostly concentrate on ideal conjugal and filial love (father-daughter, father-son, and mother-son). She listens to them repeatedly and many times a year watches public performances based on them. By the time she learns to read, she already knows the story of the pious wives Sitā and Sāvitri. In fact, in Bengal, when a girl greets her elders by touching the dust of their feet to her head, she is blessed with "Be like Sitā and Sāvitri."

Sitā, who is considered one of the most ideal of Indian women because she was a faithful, tolerant, and sacrificing wife, was a princess married to Rāma, the great hero of the epic *The Rāmāyana*. Sitā was beautiful, pious, and devoted to her husband. Her love and devotion to Rāma were tested many times. After she was abducted by the demon king Rāvana, Rāma did not wish to accept her back as his wife until she proved her chastity by standing in fire; the fire could not burn her because a chaste women has supernatural power. Later, when the pregnant Sitā had been exiled to the forest because Rāma had succumbed to his subjects' suspicions about her chastity, she withstood all such false allegations without protest. Although she grew old in banishment, she continued to love her husband and abide by his judgment. Thus Sitā was the ideal wife who was supposed to have reached the heights of conjugal love, consisting of unconditional obedience, self-sacrificing love, and tolerance. The ideal wife must accept her husband's wishes and remain faithful and devoted to him irrespective of his behavior.

The second example of idealized conjugal love comes from the epic *The Mahābhārata*. This story, which almost every girl knows by heart, is the story of the princess Sāvitri.

Sāvitri was the daughter of the king of the land Madra and grew into a beautiful, graceful, intelligent, and virtuous young woman. One day she saw Satyavān [the Truthful], the son of a blind and exiled king, and fell in love with him. She told her

father that no one but Satyavān should be her husband.
However, the great sage Nārada told her father that Satyavān
was destined to die within a year. The father tried to dissuade the
daughter, but she did not listen. She answered that a woman
can choose her husband only once and therefore she must be
married to Satyavān. After the wedding Sāvitri became a hermit,
living with her husband's family in the forest. She led the life of
an extremely pious and virtuous woman. At the end of the year
the fateful day came when her husband was to die. Sāvitri
observed a very austere ritual vow, and fasted for three days. The
last day of the fast her husband wished to go to the woods to fetch
fruit for her. Sāvitri followed. After a while, as Satyavān was
cutting a branch of a tree, he became ill and pale. Sāvitri put his
head in her lap and bravely awaited his death. Yama, the god of
death, appeared to take Satyavān's life away. But Sāvitri
followed. Yama tried to send her back, telling her she would not
gain anything by following him. Sāvitri began to converse with
Yama so intelligently and pleasantly that Yama, very pleased
with her company, wanted to give her a boon. She requested
Yama to give back her father-in-law's eyesight. It was granted.
But Sāvitri still followed and talked and was granted another
boon. She asked Yama to restore her father-in-law's kingdom to
him. It too was granted. But Sāvitri still followed. The third boon
she asked was to have a hundred children. Yama granted that
also and tried to persuade her again to leave him and go back.
Sāvitri still followed and conversed like a well-versed and highly
religious person. Yama was so pleased and impressed by her that
he even granted her last wish, which was to give her husband's
life back, so that the previous wish (to have one hundred
children) could be realized.

Because of her great perseverance in her love for her husband,
and her religious piety, Sāvitri got her dead husband's life back.
A good (faithful and pious) wife has such superhuman power.
Although *The Mahābhārata* abounds with such examples of
virtuous, powerful wives and exemplary conjugal love, it also
contains many episodes of erotic and passionate love between the
gods and the mortals (similar to the Greek and Roman legends).
These stories, however, are not related to a growing girl in a
Bengali home until she is older. The best interpretation of the
erotic love episodes in *The Mahābhārata* was done by the great
Sanskrit poet Kālidāsa. Every Bengali girl reads excerpts from

Kālidāsa's verses as part of her course work. The teacher uses these as a part of Sanskrit lessons, but stresses the stylistic and grammatical quality. At fourteen and fifteen, girls rarely overlook the content of these verses, in spite of the emphasis on style. Both Kālidāsa and Bhababhuti (the Sanskrit authors included in most school curricula) describe erotic love with exquisite beauty of language and style. The famous creations of Kālidāsa are *Śakuntalā* and *Meghdut*. Both are based on love between men and women, the latter depicting the irresistible passion of love. [8]

When a girl in her teens reads and tries to digest the excerpts from such Sanskrit authors, even though her attention is drawn to the stylistic and linguistic aspects, she cannot help noting the great passion of marital and extramarital love. In these works, unlike the epics, the moral and ethical aspect of marriage and the ideal woman's role are not emphasized. The young girl finds, in contrast to the epics, another aspect of conjugal love that seems to have existed only among Kālidāsa's and Bhababhuti's characters. She notes that the quality of the style of these great poets is captivating because the content deals with human passion rather than virtue and duty alone. Rāma's love for Sita after she was abducted by Rāvana was described by Bhababhuti as follows:

> But ah the sorrow died in me, O Lakshman,
> When I went further into the forest into Want.
> I had *Sitā!* Now it rises again
> Like fire, set swiftly blazing by the logs.
> Blow o' wind; where my beloved tarries
> Touch her feet, and then me too.
> In thee our bodies touch one another,
> In the moon our glances are united. [9]

Classical Sanskrit literature also teaches her the intensity and poignancy of another kind of love—namely, the love between father and daughter, mother and son. One of the masterpieces in Sanskrit literature is the long soliloquy of the sage Kanya when his daughter Sakuntala has to leave his āsram to be united with her husband. Every educated father and daughter in Bengal is acquainted with this part of Sakuntala's story and identifies with the father and the daughter of the story.

During this time she reads or listens to stories taken from medieval literature and may also participate in certain ritual observances (both religious and secular) based on episodes of medieval literature. She often has opportunities to watch her older female relatives' rites called *bratas*. The stories are usually based on themes such as the desirability of motherhood, and goodness in sacrificing for the welfare of one's husband. The same morals that the epics stress remain, but are couched in a more homespun form, which appeals to folk sentiment. Even a Bengali girl who is brought up in the city of Calcutta experiences such observances, either in the city if there happen to be older women in the family who are responsible for this side of Bengali tradition, or when she visits the villages when she goes on vacation. Two examples from the *brata-kathā* recipe for household rites support the above statements. One of the most popular stories is read or told by an elderly woman when she observes the rites called *Sasthi-brata*.

Sasthi is the deity of fertility whom all rural women worship. The story talks about a very lazy and unmannerly woman who did not observe wifely duties such as cleaning the house, cooking in time, and waiting for the men to come home and eat. She often ate before others and was too lazy to work. She also never bothered to worship the deity Sasthi. As a result, she never had a child who lived to grow into an adult. They all died at very early ages. After she lost several sons she dreamed one night that the deity would be appeased if she began to observe her *brata*. She did, and her next son lived and she had several children afterward.

The other very popular episode is the story of Behulā and Lakhindar.

Behulā was the ideal wife who, like Sitā, achieved the greatest honor as a devoted and faithful wife because of her perseverance and tolerance in her love for her husband. Like Sāvitri, Behulā also brought her husband's life back from the god of death because she simply did not give up. In this story, because of its folk interpretation, the emphasis is less on the ethics of conjugal love. In snake-infested lower Bengal, the primary idea is the need of worshiping the deity of snakes, Manasā. Lakhindar's father, Chānd, was a big merchant who did not believe in Manasā and thus ignored her. Manasā, in her wrath, tried to destroy him, first by ruining his fortune and then by sending a snake to kill his only son on the very night of his son's wedding to Behulā. Chānd still did not bend, but Manasā was appeased by Behulā's penance and devotion in her love for her husband as shown by the fact that, determined not to give up, she traveled to the world of death with her husband's dead body.

There are days in the ritual calendar of Bengal when these tales (*kathā*) are related by the older women in the home to the younger girls who sit nearby and listen attentively. The girls also watch their elders observe the rites with flowers, sandalwood paste, incense, effigies, and pictures. Listening to such stories, with their overtone of ethical content, creates a religious feeling. The young girl learns that it must be good to have children and love one's husband, as Sāvitri and Behulā did, and that a lazy and greedy woman loses her children because the deity of fertility does not bless her. She further feels these rites must be effective since all women, including her grandmother, are observing them.

These folk rituals or *bratas* also express a wish to be fulfilled in the future. For example, Sasthi is worshiped so that a barren woman may be blessed with children. One very popular *brata*, observed by unmarried girls in Bengal who wish to acquire a good husband like the god Śiva, is called *Śiva-rātrir brata* (the rite of the night of Śiva). The girls fast all day and in the evening collect in a Śiva temple to offer food and other gifts to his *lingam* while praying to be blessed by a husband like him. Almost every Bengali girl who has not been totally uprooted from her culture knows this rite and is thrilled about observing it before she is married. Even the girls living in Calcutta and attending colleges believe in such observances.

One of my informants who has a B.A. degree from a college in Calcutta responded in the following way:

Oh yes, I observed the *Śiva-rātri* twice. Once when I was visiting my mother's mother in her village forty miles from the city, grandmother asked me if I would like to join the other girls in the neighborhood in observing the Śiva-rātri. I was eighteen at that time, studying in the second year of college. I thought it would be fun. Also, let me admit, something told me it might be a good idea in view of my future. Perhaps, I would turn out to have a good husband. At least there was no harm. It was hard to fast all day because I was not used to it. The village girls fast so often on some occasion or other. I was quite weak by the end of the day; but I enjoyed it thoroughly. At nightfall when ten of us gathered at the Śiva temple in the village I felt very religious and pious. I prayed very seriously. . . . The second time was here in Calcutta when I was a third-year student and was staying in the college dorm. Someone in our class, I forget who now, started the idea and about fifteen of us got interested in observing the rite. We talked to the matron-warden, and she was quite happy to hear that we "modern" girls were not totally spoiled. In fact she made all the arrangements so that we could observe the rite as authentically as possible. She even arranged for a special menu for us after we broke the fast. Some girls, especially the very fasionable ones, joked and taunted about it because the *brata* was for the purpose of acquiring a Śiva-like husband. One girl, I remember, came up to me and said that she would not even like to accept Śiva as a husband because Śiva was too unpredictable and unglamorous for her. She would much rather observe a *brata* to get hold of someone like Uttam Kumar [the matinee idol of the Bengali screen]. . . . If you ask me whether I believed in the whole thing, I have no answer. I liked doing it and, unlike my friend who jeered about it, I felt good in doing it. I always liked Śiva, and knowing the story of Śiva and Umā I thought a marriage like that would not be bad.

I did not ask her if she thought her penance was really answered by Śiva.

Young girls, irrespective of their sociocultural background, are given such ideals. Śiva, who is a very unusual god in the sense that he does not go by the usual conventions of the Hindu pantheon, is unconcerned with household details. He is withdrawn and indifferent. But he is very faithful as a lover, as a husband. He may be considered the antithesis of Krishna, the god of love, who is attractive, playful, mischievous, and deluding, but irresistible to women. A girl is blessed by her elders when they say "May your husband be like Śiva."

A third class of medieval literature is most significant to a young girl's imagination: Vaishnava poetry and the associated forms of performing arts based on the *Krishna lila* and *bhakti*. If the impact of the folk rituals and tales makes her aware of her household duties, ideal roles, and so on, Vaishnava poetry takes her away from the household to the realm of imagination and romance.

In Bengal the most widely read Vaishnava poems were written by three local poets, Chandidās, Gobindadās, and Vidyāpati (fifteenth century). These poets, who were born in rural Bengal and who wrote for the village people, use symbols and images directly from the rural scene. As a result the theme of love between Rādhā and the god Krishna is mixed with folk eros and deep religious emotion (*bhakti*). The best example of this is the *Krishna Kirtan* by Chandidās. People who read and reread the verses about the divine love between Rādhā and Krishna readily identify with them, not always because of pure religious feelings but often for the vicarious pleasure derived from the stories. Both Vidyāpati and Chandidās display a knowledge of the workings of a lover's heart, and portray them feelingly and minutely—the first trembling impressions of love, the resistless force of its influence, the bitter pains of separation and jealousy, the working of hope, the effects of despair. The excerpts below, translated by Edward C. Dimock, Jr., and Denise Levertov[10] from Vidyāpati and Chandidās express the above moods.

He [Krishna] speaks:

Her slender body like a flash of lightning,
her feet, color of dawn, stepping swiftly
among the other lotus petals. . . .
Friend, tell me who she is! She plays
among her friends,
plays with my heart.
When she raises her eyebrows I see
the arching waves of the River Kālindī.

Rādhā describes the depth of her love:

As water to sea creatures,
moon nectar to *chakora* birds,
companionable dark to the stars—
my love is to Krishna.

My body hungers for his
as mirror image hungers
for twin of flesh

His life cuts into my life
as the stain of the moon's rabbit
engraves the moon.

A girl in a Bengali home is not exposed to such Vaishnava poetry until she is in college, when it is included in her vernacular courses as part of "The History of Bengali Literature," or "Contemporary Bengali Literature." She is instructed to read them in order to evaluate their literary significance and the social conditions of the time of their writing. However, no matter how academic the understanding is, these verses easily catch her imagination. She cannot help appreciating the ecstatic love Rādhā felt for Krishna, even though some of the symbols and expressions may not be as familiar to her as they would be if she were closely acquainted with the rural scene. What is lost in the classroom discussion is compensated for in other ways. From the time she is a little girl, she has the opportunity to watch folk plays, musicals, and operas. These folk operas use repeatedly the same theme of *Krishna līlā*. Nothing is more popular on the folk stage than the theme of Rādhā's love for Krishna and the agony she suffers because of it. She may also read this poetry with her father or elder brothers if the latter happen to be interested in literature as a subject.

She also watches the Vaishnavis (the young female devotees of the Vaishnava cult) who wander from door to door for alms in their saffron saris and sing verses such as the above. These women, often recruited from the lower castes, are young widows who prefer to spend their lives worshiping the lord Krishna and feeling divine love rather than be concubines, prostitutes, or cooks in wealthier households. A young Vaishnavi, dressed in saffron with sandalwood decoration on her face and body, bead necklaces made of wood from the basil plant, playing a one-string violin or a pair of cymbals and singing verses depicting the agony and pleasure of Rādhā's love, has a very strong influence on a girl of tender age. The impact is greater than that of a classroom lecture of a professor who discusses the beauty of Vaishnava literature. The girl may even feel a strong desire to identify with this young devotee who has a religious and sacred aura about her that is generated by her total abandonment to love for the god and identification with Rādhā. (According to the Vaishnava cult every devotee, male or female, must identify with Rādhā to feel love and devotion for Krishna.)

A girl also has opportunities to watch folk theater, operas, and musicals based on the theme of *Krishna lilā*. These operas and musicals are staged by established theatrical companies who travel throughout the state, setting up temporary stages in the middle of villages or parks of big cities, usually for several days during religious festivals. While not all the operas are based on *Krishna lilā*, none is more popular. [11]

Here one needs to pay attention to a seeming dichotomy between the ideal husband image, Śiva, and the ideal lover image, Krishna, both of which are imprinted on a Bengali girl's mind from very early in her life. This ideal of husband-lover, based on religious literature and rituals, is extremely important. The problem becomes one not only of opposition, but also contradiction, because a woman is encouraged to worship equally both gods, Śiva the ascetic and Krishna the libertine. The attraction of both is great.

The central theme of *Śiva-Purānas* reflects the basic conflict of Indian culture from Vedic times, namely the conflict between asceticism and eroticism. Śiva, because of his ascetic aspect (which is supposed to create an invulnerability to desire), causes Pārvati, his wife, to desire him all the more. Śiva admits that his destruction of Kāma (god of love) has merely added to Kāma's power over him. Pārvati's attraction for Śiva is unconventional. [12] There lies the ambiguous nature of Śiva's appeal, and Śiva is considered an ascetic and a householder par excellence. This is the Śiva a Bengali girl worships in her adolescence while she observes *Śiva-ratrir brata* and wishes for a husband like him whom Pārvati desired and obtained through penance and seduction. The Krishna myth, as interpreted by the Vaishnava literature, pictures Krishna as the cowherd lover whose aim is to propagate passion as the symbol of final union with God. The function of Krishna according to Vaishnava poetry seems to be to defend two theses, (1) that romantic love is the most exalted experience in life, and (2) that of all the roads to salvation, the impassioned adoration (*bhakti*) of God is the most valid.

Krishna, either in the ritual practice of Bengali women or in their fantasies, never comes to take the figure of a husband—a desirable man to marry. It is Rādhā's burning and consuming love for her lover outside her marriage, that Vaishnava poetry so well expresses, that moves a growing girl. Her tender age blooming to womanhood identifies with Rādhā and longs for similar ecstasy. Such an identification is achieved without difficulty because of the additional help of other arts, which are often based on the theme of Rādhā's love for irresistible Krishna.

Interestingly enough, the same Śiva-Krishna dichotomy is also emphasized by later literature, but through different imagery and symbols, as we shall see later in this chapter.

Going back for a moment to the daily activities of the young girl, often in late afternoons she may be asked to accompany one of her older aunts (who is less addicted to noon naps) to visit a neighbor. There she may have a chance to sit with them and overhear the conversation. They talk about their families, their worries over marriages to be arranged for growing teenagers, complaints against daughters-in-law or sisters-in-law, and so on. They also discuss which woman in the neighborhood may be expecting a baby, who is going to see a doctor because of some unknown disease, and so on.

During the late afternoon, when the girl comes back from her social visits with her grandmother or aunt, she may be summoned to help one of her older sisters serve tea to the family. She may take the tray out to the living room to serve the men and their guests. This is good for her, she is told; she learns how to serve food to men, something she will have to do most of her married life. Other than this, her contact with the kitchen is minimal at this age (between eight and ten years).

Once or twice a week, in the evenings, she may have to accompany one of the older aunts or the grandmother to religious meetings or a temple. At eight or ten she may have an option to decline and stay home for her schoolwork or music lessons.

It is a common belief in such households that a girl must acquire some musical skills as part of her endowments for marriageability. Beginning around eight or ten, she takes lessons from a young male teacher, and later, by the time she is fourteen to fifteen, she may go to a music school to specialize in learning a particular type of song or instrument. To be able to sing a number of devotional songs or songs by Tagore or to be able to play the sitar moderately well is considered a definite point in her favor when negotiations for marriage begin, though she may never be encouraged to cultivate such skills after she is married. She also takes these lessons to please her grandfather and uncles, who once in a while like to listen to a devotional song or two. [13] She may also be called by one of the older women to sing in the family shrine while the offering takes place.

The subject matter of these devotional songs is *bhakti* (devotion) in a woman for her god (Vishnu or Krishna) to whom she dedicates her life and soul. For example, the words of these songs often run like the following: "Oh my God, my master, my life craves to be one with you/The world has no attraction for me. . . ." Both melody and lyric are very moving, and it is not rare that the women have tears in their eyes when they listen to the girl sing. This gives the girl a thrill and satisfaction, and while singing them she herself may feel some sort of exalted feeling.

She also learns how to sing Tagore's songs, which deal with a vast range of moods and feelings. She likes to sing those of Tagore's songs that accurately describe her own feelings to herself or to her friends. [14] Or perhaps she likes to imagine that her feelings are like those the poet describes so movingly and beautifully. She is also taught a number of so-called modern songs (usually movie hits) that deal with romantic love between a man and a woman, usually the types one sees in the movies or reads about in popular novels. The common theme is unfulfilled love, promised and never returned. Consequently, the lyric is full of pathos expressed by such words as death, sorrow, memory. Most of these songs can perhaps be composed by a permutation and combination of three words, namely, "I," "you," and "love." She learns to sing them primarily because of the enthusiasm of her music teacher, who is appointed by the family to teach her devotional songs; but the teacher finds it boring to concentrate on that theme alone. The girl does not mind either, especially if the teacher is young and good-looking and sings with a lot of feeling. She can imagine that some of these deep sighs in the songs may well be directed to her by the teacher himself. Indeed this may happen. Nevertheless, she does not think such indirect approaches are conscious on the teacher's part. So the matter does not go beyond this level.

Be that as it may, the music lessons and the songs themselves give some food for her emotional needs. She finds it satisfactory to hum them to herself off and on, because the words do express something she likes to think is true about herself. Often they express an unknown longing for a nameless, shapeless emotion that she later learns to call "love" (*prem*).

At school there take place occasional extracurricular activities, so-called cultural functions.[15] She may take part in them, in a small role in a drama or in a dancing recital. The dramas are based on either Sanskrit texts or Tagore's writings. A girl is very much encouraged to participate in such performances, which the parents and relatives attend. The women in the family continue to talk about the excellent performance their little daughter put on and how beautiful she looked in makeup on the stage. She herself enjoys acting and participating in such functions because, apart from being the center of attraction, she also lives through her stage roles for a while.

Case no. 11: When I was asked by the headmistress to play the role of Surupa in *Chitrāngadā*[16] for the foundation day of school, I was very happy because they chose me out of all the girls. We had rehearsals every day for a couple of hours, and I looked forward to this. During the three evenings that we staged the dance-drama, I nearly forgot who I was. I began to feel like Surupa and while dancing in front of Arjuna, the hero, I felt I really loved him. The role of Arjuna was played by one of my very close girl friends and this made little difference. She looked like a very handsome prince with makeup and I could not think of her as anything but Arjuna, whom I was supposed to love and please in my role. This feeling grew over the days of rehearsal and became climactic when we really performed the play. I remember clearly on the last day, that, while coming home after the performance with my father, who picked me up from the school, I did not want to take off my makeup. I lingered for several hours and watched myself in the mirror. I was amazed at my own beauty. I wished and almost felt I was Surupa. Too bad, such feelings do not last too long.

If she goes to an English-medium convent school, she may also play the roles of Juliet, Portia, or Desdemona in her annual school functions.

This kind of authorized encouragement of artistic talent, however, is limited to school performances that only occur two or three times a year. The distinction between occasional institutionalized artistic endeavor and concentrated cultivation toward an artistic profession is a very definite one. While the former is considered part of her training, the latter is quite unacceptable for a girl of good breeding and upbringing. [17]

In her adolescence, both within her school/college curricula and without, she is encouraged to read a great variety of material, including the following:

Indian (Bengali)
Classical: Pieces from the Hindu epics *The Rāmāyana* and *The Mahābhārata*; romantic and erotic literature of the period c. A.D. 400. Important authors: Kālidāsa and Bhababhuti.
Medieval: Mangal Kābya; folk ritual or *brata-kathā*; Vaishnava poetry.
Modern: Bengal renaissance literature with a romantic tradition influenced by the west. Important authors: Bankim Chandra Chatterjee, Rabindranath Tagore, Sarat Chandra Chatterjee. Post-Tagore: The era of the "New Wave."
Journals and magazines: Monthly and weekly.
Mass Media: Religious dramas, recitals, music conferences based on the same themes from classical and medieval literature. Movies, plays, dance-dramas, ballets, based on both classical and modern literature.

Western [18]
Classical and Italian: Legends of Greece and Rome; Dante.
Renaissance: Shakespeare.
Romantic: Shelley, Keats, Byron, Wordsworth.
The French naturalistic and realistic novelists: Zola, Flaubert.
Modern and popular: Jane Austen, Maugham, Hemingway, A. J. Cronin.
Mass media: Movies from America, primarily Hollywood love stories, such as *Gone with the Wind, Roman Holiday, For Whom the Bell Tolls.* Plays staged by traveling companies performing Shakespeare in the big cities only.

Let me at this stage comment on the nature of the modern Bengali literature that an upper-class Bengali girl is exposed to both in high school and at home; she continues to read them even after she is married. In what follows I shall select only the most prominent and widely read authors who, while influencing women's fantasies, also are good observers of women in this culture.

The Bengali literary tradition of the nineteenth century was influenced by a romanticism that has its roots neither in Indian classical literature nor in medieval folk eroticism. [19] This romanticism followed the European tradition of post-renaissance romanticism. The man who introduced into Bengali literature this new romantic tradition, which eventually changed not only the literature but also the thoughts and feelings of the readers, was Bankim Chandra Chatterjee (1838–94). [20]

Bankim first expressed the beginning of the realization of romantic love between men and women, a new brand of romantic love (*prem*) as more than simply erotic lust (*kām*) that some of the classical Sanskrit literature and most of the medieval literature of secular Bengal illustrate profusely. [21] This new attitude toward love between men and women shook the foundation of the stereotyped male-female relationship that continued to persist and be supported by a male-oriented social system. Nirad C. Chaudhury in his *Bangalir Jibane Ramani* (*Women in the Lives of Bengalis*, 1970) aptly describes this transplantation of western romantic love to Bengali soil. [22]

Since the social condition in Bengal was not yet appropriate for the acceptance of such ideas of love, Bankim had to create imaginary situations based in part on historical events and placed in historically remote settings. In order to elevate the relationship between men and women to the level of romantic love, he also had to pay special attention to the concept of the beauty of women, which, as in the romantic tradition of Europe, became mingled with the beauty of nature. In fact, one may argue that without the conscious appreciation of the vast rivers, green woods, and vast stretches of paddy fields this new expression of love for women could not have been expressed in local symbols. It was made easier because in Indian thinking women have always been identified with nature. [23] A woman's beauty and the beauty of Bengali nature became one in the imagination of Bankim, whose novel *Kapalakundala* expresses this ideal. [24] The second thing that influenced the Bengali attitude toward women had to do with Bankim's attempt to introduce the concept of respect for a woman one can both love and desire. The third characteristic feature in Bankim's newly created image of love has roots in both the European romantic tradition and in the Indian religious tradition. He was influenced by the divine quality of intense love that often comes from the separation of the lover and the beloved. The fourth contribution that Bankim made was his successful attempt to bring together the classical idea of a woman's chastity and devotion in conjugal love. In classical literature both were emphasized separately, the latter often at the expense of the former. Bankim, for the first time, combined them to emphasize the fact that romantic love can be realized in an ideally created conjugal love if strengthened by a woman's devotion and her chastity.

Bankim was the first to introduce into Bengali literature both the concept of romantic love and the changed concept of women. Both were successfully introduced because of his great talent, assisted by the socio-political milieu of Bengal at that time. British rule was at its peak, and western education spreading, effectively offering complementary support for these concepts through the western literature included in school and college curricula. Nonetheless, the ideas were not accepted readily. A very strong opposition came from male-dominated orthodox Hindu society, which felt that Bankim's writings would corrupt the women by this changed attitude toward them. But precisely because of this viewpoint women began to read him avidly. [25] In every middle- and upper middle-class Bengali home a girl has access to the volumes of Bankim's work. He is included as well in high school and college courses.

Two other authors are also significant for present purposes. They came after Bankim and picked up certain trends from him. They continued to emphasize both romantic love and the changed image of women. One is the Nobel laureate poet and philosopher Rabindranath Tagore (1861–1941). The other is Sarat Chandra Chatterjee (1876–1938). Tagore, who influenced Bengali culture more than any other individual, may be considered the major phenomenon behind the twentieth-century renaissance in Bengal. His writings continued to emphasize both divine and romantic love, but moved it from imaginary and historical settings to a semi-urban milieu. (He lived most of his life in Calcutta.) He often put a woman and a man side by side and for the first time introduced the concept of friendship between a man and a woman who can work together, respect each other, and also be involved in a romantic relationship. Tagore more than anyone tried to break the stereotype of the dichotomous image that a Bengali man has regarding a woman— a respectable mother and a desirable sex-object. Tagore tried to create his woman as a total person who is a combination of mother, wife, friend and mistress. [26]

Some of his short stories have their settings in rural Bengal where the abundance of large rivers, storms, monsoon, autumn skies, and green paddy fields mingle with the love for women, love between friends, and so on. His novels deal with the conflict within individuals, the new image of women, and the conditioning of urban life that stifles the open generosity of rural nature. A good example is his short novel *Nastanir* (The Damaged Nest).

The heroine, a sensitive, educated, upper-class woman, suffers from an internal conflict between her romantic needs and her duty to love her husband, who obviously is not satisfying such needs. Her husband, who is very kind, is always busy with his press and publishing business and has little time for her. She has no children or housework to keep her busy. She reads a lot of Bankim and other authors, including Tagore, and becomes bored and lonely. Her husband's cousin comes to visit them, and she showers her affection, love, and attention on him. He is her only companion. Their friendship, which takes on a very strong romantic overtone, awakens her emotionally, and she is able to live fully and happily for the first time in her life. The cousin appreciates her affection and love for him, and responds. The story ends with the cousin leaving for his higher studies in England, and the husband and wife finding themselves in an empty world with a gap between them.

This short novel depicts a familial and psychological situation in which a woman becomes romantically involved with a relative of her husband (see chap. 3). It also illustrates a new trend in literature; an author is courageous enough to recognize with insight and understanding such emotional conditioning and conflicts within a woman. Tagore is also the first writer who brought his women out of the kitchen and bedroom and into the parlor where they argue with men and exchange ideas while still remaining very feminine. He also has written a number of satirical pieces in which he shows how the whole new concept of "falling in love" can be ill-digested by Bengali youth. Some of his men appear to be weak and cowardly, lacking responsibility or the courage to love and respect a woman.

His stories of conjugal love deal with similar insight and understanding in the psychodynamics of marital relationships. His portrayal of a woman's inner conflicts attained a level that was totally new in Bengali literature. A few examples:

A short story entitled "Paylā Nambar" (Number One) revolves around a professor's wife who makes tea and snacks for his colleagues and students. She is weary of this role and seeks a new identity. Her neighbor, a young man who notices her and understands her situation, feels sympathetic and is attracted to her. He offers to rescue her from this meaningless existence and promises a better life. She refuses him and defies both the husband and the promised lover because of the fear of encountering the same fate again.

In the story "Aparichita" (The Unknown Woman), after the marriage negotiation has been broken off over a disagreement between the two families on the amount of dowry, the woman accidentally meets her would-have-been husband on a trip. She feels very close and tender toward him. She makes believe that she is living as the ideal good wife for the satisfaction of her own self-image, even though the wedding has not taken place.

The story "Dristidan" (The Offering of Eyesight) also deals with the complexity of a woman's love within the frame of ideal conjugal love. The wife in this story goes blind; since she loves her husband very strongly and wishes not to deprive him of all the marital pleasures, she makes a great sacrifice by requesting him to remarry. Her pains are compensated for by the pride and satisfaction she receives from being a martyr. She thus becomes an ideal wife in the eyes of others and herself. Later she becomes heartbroken when she finds out that her husband has deceived her through lies. Her love for her husband is shattered when she can no longer respect him.

Ghare Bāire (The Home and the World) is a novel in which the heroine is caught between duty and love toward her Śiva-like husband and attraction and infatuation for her Krishna-like lover. The setting of the story is the chaotic social situation during the time of the freedom movement. The woman is childless and very intelligent. She spends a lot of time with her husband and his friends arguing and discussing social and political problems. The friend of the husband is a terrorist deeply involved in the movement and treats her with great admiration and devotion. He treats her like a goddess and identifies her with the motherland. She is overwhelmed by this attraction and attention, for her husband is always quiet and withdrawn, though affectionate, without much expression.

This novel is significant because it suggests not only the inner conflict of a woman in relation to the Śiva-Krishna dichotomy but also the attitude toward women of a Bengali man of a particular sociocultural background. A wife can be visualized as the mother and the country itself. She is the source of power, *shakti*, to inspire the men. While the husband emphasizes her role as housewife and companion, his very eloquent, aggressive friend emphasizes her image as the powerful goddess who cannot be, and ought not to be, satisfied with the role of a housewife alone, but who should inspire all the men toward their mission—to free the motherland. The unhappiness of the heroine is based on the conflict between two kinds of expectations, these two roles her husband and her admirer impose on her.

A girl in a Bengali home begins to read Tagore's short stories and novels by the time she is fourteen or fifteen and continues to read them while concurrently taking in a number of plays, dance-dramas, and movies based on his stories. Girls who have talent for singing, dancing, or acting perform in these dramas and identify very strongly with their roles. Although a girl of fifteen may find it difficult to grasp and identify with Tagore's sophisticated treatment of a woman's inner psychology, she nevertheless becomes aware of such complexities and this sharpens her sensitivity and understanding of a woman's feelings.

The third author that a woman reads is Sarat Chandra Chatterjee. She not only reads Sarat, but also identifies closely with his female characters. There is perhaps not one middle-class Bengali woman with some education who does not read Sarat over and over again, weeping and laughing with his characters. Sarat is the first and most effective of sympathetic writers, since he treats women with sympathy and understanding; but he also puts them on pedestals to honor and worship. If Tagore takes his women out of the kitchen and puts them in living rooms, Sarat takes his women out of kitchen and courtyard and puts them inside temples to be deified.

Sarat's novels are written about (and for) the suffering women of rural Bengal, as opposed to Tagore's semi-urban women. At the turn of the century, conservative Brahmanical Hinduism encouraged a tyrannical, male-dominated society. Sarat rejected women's roles determined by such conservative attitudes and protested through his novels, as can be seen in the major theme of his works, the conflict between women's cultural norms and personal aspirations. This he shows through a realistic portrayal of the suffering in a woman's everyday life. Nowhere can women better recognize themselves than in the pages of his novels, where every woman finds an agonizing conflict between her personal ideals and her social role. His sympathy with the women he created makes them noble and powerful; and this has tremendous attraction for his female readers. His women are admirable because of their qualities of sacrifice, tolerance, and devotion in their love for their husbands (and lovers) and children. These values, which are completely in tune with social ideals, make the woman's position even more pathetic when male society does not offer her due recognition and respect. A sympathetic description, highlighting this discrepancy, can create a dramatic effect of pity and helplessness with which a woman reader can easily identify. She can project her life situation (even though the real life situations may not always be parallel) upon the condition of the women in the story, and can enjoy the satisfaction generated by pride in the author's recognition of her strength and greatness. At least one male member of her society gives her recognition and credit. Sarat Chandra's women, who become respected models because they are suffering and never attain happiness in their personal lives, encourage women readers to accept their own misery. Such a reader gathers that she does not lose by sacrificing herself and by tolerating the willfulness of men for the sake of love. The more she suffers, the more power she acquires as a woman of virtue, and it is her fate to endure this discrepancy between her social role and her personal ideal.

Two women from Sarat Chandra's widely read novels might be described here.

The first one, Roma, is a village widow, hence not permitted to live a normal life like a married woman. Her calf love for Romesh, whom she knew in elementary school, is not allowed to blossom. Roma's life is a long process of adjustment to conservative village social norms, which suppress in her all desire for personal happiness. Society does not relinquish its norms, and even Romesh does not openly acknowledge her silent love and devotion to him. Roma is left with no consolation.

This is a case of total martyrdom on the part of a widow in a tyrannical Hindu village society. Roma stands for a woman who suffers because of her social condition and because of her natural desire to love. When they read this novel, *Pally Samāj* (The Village Society), many women, whether of rural or urban background, shed tears for her tragedy.

The second woman is Annadadidi who suffers not because of her socially unacceptable love, but because of her socially acceptable love for her husband, who is unworthy of such great love. Her total absorption in her husband makes her unhappy to such an extent that the ideal of conjugal love cannot satisfy her any longer. She has no alternative but to step out of her ideal role and try to find satisfaction where she can by indulging in extramarital affairs. Consequently social judgment is harsh. Annadadidi fails despite her attempt to play her role completely. Again a woman becomes a victim of irreversible tragedy.

Another novel of Sarat Chandra's, *Grihadāha* (The Burning of the Home), also can be mentioned at this point. This book, the title of which has the same implication as *Nastanir* (The Damaged Nest), deals with the psychological conflict of a woman who must determine her allegiance to one of the two types of men in her life: the quiet, apparently indifferent, ascetic, but stable, husband and the restless, attentive, exciting, but unstable, lover. This novel, which is similar to Tagore's *Ghare Bāire*, describes the conflict very poignantly. The heroine is torn between a Śiva-like husband and a Krishna-like admirer. She is frustrated by a husband who is emotionally distant yet admirable and by a lover who is not admirable but emotionally very close.

Both Tagore and Sarat Chandra highlighted the self-centered nature of husbands who do not care to demonstrate or express their love for their wives. Despite their apparent dependability, Bengali husbands fail to offer the emotional security a woman in love requires.

The frustration generated in a woman by the conflict between the Śiva and Krishna models both Tagore and Sarat Chandra, and many later writers in Bengal, express; even though emotional conflict is universal, it becomes extremely significant for a Bengali woman because of her dual allegiance to two models— Śiva and Krishna—reinforced by religious ideals and myths.

Sarat Chandra is also eloquent when dealing with the ideal of motherhood in this culture. In *Pally Samāj*, the conservative, male-dominated village society cruelly denies any consideration to the young widow, but it pays heed to the matron-mother Vishweswari, who criticizes their attitude. By elevating the ten-year-old Mādhabi, who showed selfless affection to someone else's son, the author strongly supports the cultural ideal. He declares in his novel *Srikānta*: ". . . like romantic love, mother-hood is also an inherent basic need of a woman and a woman can easily find this fulfillment even without biological motherhood."

Bankim, Tagore, and Sarat are representative of renaissance Bengali literature and from the viewpoint of this book, very important indeed. All three deal competently with the emotional conflicts and needs of Bengali women of the upper and upper middle classes. All three are not only widely read by women, but also highly recommended in high school and college curricula. A woman is considered ill-educated if she does not read the works of Sarat and Bankim, at least.

All three authors provide themes for Bengali movies, plays, and radio programs. No plot on the Bengali screen can insure box-office success as easily as a story by Sarat Chandra. The appeal is absolute and universal.

The literature that grew up after the triad of Bankim-Tagore-Sarat reflects the influence of the west, especially western European literature of the postwar period. Most of the authors remained the followers of the Tagore school, with variations in more realistic style and in the emphasis on social issues. Annadashankar Roy, for example, deals with upper middle-class men and women with great sophistication in posing the problems these characters face.

One of his heroines (in a novel in five volumes published around 1940) is a young woman from an upper-class home. She was brought up in a household staffed by maids and servants and under the indulgent and affectionate protection of a father who is educated, wealthy, and westernized. The father chooses a very bright young man for his daughter to marry, and the young woman, who never learned to refuse her father's wishes, finds herself married to a childlike, unconcerned, but intellectually oriented husband who believes in giving her equal rights and friendly treatment but no love. The young man is much involved in his pursuit of knowledge (he had always been a bright student), based on western thinking, and he does not support the Indian system of arranged marriage. He gave in because his father promised him a study-trip to England. He tells his wife that he can not love her just because she has become his wife—a situation created by their fathers. His wife begins to love him just because he is her husband. Despite her exposure to western education, she is a Hindu woman who learns also to love/worship her husband. She also likes him because of his progressive ideas about human equality—ideals that her father has taught her to respect. The husband leaves her behind for his study-trip to England where he believes he can be free of his superstitious Indian upbringing. He continues to treat her in a most civil manner without realizing her emotional need to be loved. The wife, after a while, tries to idealize her unrequited love for her husband and gradually tries to find solace in religion. She becomes deeply involved with her god/lover Krishna, a substitute for her husband. This feverish involvement with a god (which betrays both her westernized father and her husband's ideas) lasts until the day she is shocked out of this by the crude physical advances of another Krishna disciple. Her frustration with religious involvement brings her back to her father's agnostic rational world again. But her father's affection alone cannot satisfy her restlessness and desire to love and be loved by her husband with total abandon.

Annadashankar beautifully describes this dilemma—an educated woman who has strong roots in Hindu culture despite the western influence of her father. She learns to respect theoretically the ideas and thinking of both her father and her husband, but she finds happiness only in an engrossing and dedicated love that she so fruitlessly cherishes for her husband/god. Although the author's primary intention is to deal with the confusion a modern Bengali young man faced during that period of history (1935–45) because of his sincere attraction to western intellectualism in opposition to his traditional Indian upbringing (symbolized by the counter-hero) the novel also presents the problem of the inner needs of a modern woman.

More examples can be added from a group of highly talented writers of the forties and the fifties who had a strong allegiance to both European literary tradition and the legacy of Bankim, Tagore, and Sarat.

The era following Bankim-Tagore-Sarat, also known as the era of the New Wave (*Kallol Jug*), was headed by a group of talented and bold young men in Calcutta. Some of them deliberately tried to get away from the sentimentality of writing of soothing nature and beauty and wrote instead of naked desire and passion. Like the French naturalists and realists, these authors shocked their readers by deliberately breaking down the ideals of motherhood and conjugal love (a young man desires his friend's mother, a middle-aged woman involves herself in extramarital affairs). Despite their high stylistic quality, these stories gained popularity with only a limited group of intellectuals. When out-of-the-way themes began to appear, women who read them developed the attitude that the characters in such stories were exceptional people, perhaps like the avant-garde authors themselves. One young woman, who has a B.A. degree in literature and two school-age children, told me the following:

Oh yes, I read whatever I find. But let me add, most of the stories
written by the moderns do not give me the satisfaction I still
derive from reading Bankim and Tagore, for example. These
modern stories are often unreal, and it seems to me as if the
authors are trying to shock us. Sometimes they are so vulgar and
obscene that I wonder if they should not try their hands at pure
pornography. I am really careful about what my twelve-year-old
daughter reads. I don't mind if she picks up these books later, but
not at this tender age. All these authors disrupt our age-old ideals.
They are trying to turn Calcutta into Paris.

   Bengali literature following the revolution of the "New Wave"
(1950) seems to show a revival of the theme of ideal social roles,
though with more sophistication in psychological treatment.
Some authors begin to write about women beyond youth—the
frustrations of a middle-aged mother with her children grown,
and so on. The theme of becoming involved with a guru at an age
when worldly involvement becomes burdensome has always been
prevalent in this literature, although no writer dealt clearly with
the psychological ramifications of such an involvement for a
middle-aged woman. [27]
   Another literary mode that women between the ages of
fourteen and fifty habitually read includes "ladies' " magazines
and movie magazines. They cater to relatively less-educated
semi-urban and rural women and include subjects as diverse as
cooking recipes and international politics. Below is a summary of
one issue of *Mahilā* (Ladies). [28]

Short articles on Indian classical dancing, with illustrations.
Short articles on travel to a number of pilgrim centers written
      by women.
Short stories: one on the theme of marital problems in which the
      heroine is trying to convince her girl friend that legal
      separation is the only solution; one on sexual exploitation by
      the boss of a private company; one on love between a poor
      man's son and a rich man's daughter.
One detective story.
Three reports of interviews with well-known female movie stars,
      emphasizing their modest and pleasant personalities despite
      ambitious pursuit of a career.

A regular column of questions and answers on minor medical problems mostly concerned with sexual matters.
Articles on cooking, embroidery, and sewing, with illustrations.
Three cartoons concerned with a husband's "change of heart."

The movie magazines are the most popular. Apart from including gossip about the lives and scandals of the stars, they also include novelettes of sentimental romantic love. These magazines are as popular among fifty-year-olds as among fifteen-year-olds. They are read and loaned continually to sisters-in-law, next-door neighbors, and even friends across town and form part of the pattern of afternoon gossip sessions, naps, and movies. They supply vicarious pleasure and the illusion of sharing the glamorous lives of movie stars and other popular heroines who live in a fortunate household where the husband writes poetry about the beauty of his wife and brings home jasmine flowers for her to use in decorating her long black hair. The married women devour such articles and short stories because they offer the promise of some sort of a dream world of fulfilled expectations. The same is true for the popular movies in which every young couple eventually achieves a happy life, or a woman becomes the victim of a tragic separation from her lover, son, or husband. Such a woman—and there are many in Bengali movies—continues to sacrifice, weep, and sing sentimental songs of love. The female audience escapes for three hours into such a world, and it is plausible that they come out feeling partially reconciled to woman's ever-sacrificing roles as wife, mother, and lover.

I must mention a few women authors in this connection. Ashapurna Devi and Pratibha Bose, two of the most popular among women readers, write novels and short stories similar to those by Sarat Chandra. They write about wives of upper-class and middle-class homes who are always exploited both physically and emotionally by men. The women readers of these novels, written by women about women, are deeply moved. Ashapurna Devi's novels, which emphasize the glory of conjugal love in an urban setting, are frequently given to a bride as wedding presents. They have attractive jackets, often with illustrations of a demure wife touching the feet of her husband to show her respect. Narratives of deep conjugal love lie on the table next to the nuptial bed, perhaps in symbolic compensation for the frustrations of actual experience.

A Bengali girl in school or college is also exposed to some examples of western literature. During her last years in high school, a schoolgirl reads selections from Shakespeare and from some nineteenth-century poets, Wordsworth, Shelley, Keats, Byron, and so on. She also reads the legends of Greece and Rome and finds a similarity between the gods of Hindu mythology and those of the Greek. With their emphasis on love, hate, and revenge, they all seem very human to her. In their romantic exploits, Krishna and the Greek god Apollo appear very similar. The schoolgirl may also read, in an abbreviated version, of Dante's divine love for Beatrice and compare it to Bankim's *Krishnakantha's Will* in which the hero talks about the peace to be found in divine love.

While these books are in her school and college courses (and the selection of items remained more or less the same during the adolescent years of the women I studied), she may also do some extracurricular reading in English. During her long summer and autumn vacations and the time she spends awaiting her final exam results, she may read a few popular English or American authors. These books are usually given to her by her friends or elder siblings. She has greater access to them if she happens to have friends with strong western backgrounds or have attended English schools or have brothers or fathers with foreign degrees. Although her identification with the female characters in English and American novels is not complete because of the differences in sociocultural settings, she finds these characters extremely thrilling to read about. She may even have daydreams about lovers who look and behave like foreign heroes who appear so fascinating and unattainable. If, in special circumstances, a girl comes in contact with a man of another culture, her romantic involvement may be very strong (see Case no. 13, pp. 63–64).

This is also the time before her marriage when she goes with friends from high school and college to see Hollywood movies. If she is in a small town her opportunities of seeing foreign films may be limited to once a month or so. These movies, which complement and correspond to her extracurricular readings, are romantic and sentimental. They may also be wholesome love stories with the usual matinee idols: *Roman Holiday, For Whom the Bell Tolls, Gone With the Wind.*

A girl of twenty who is attending a university in Calcutta and majoring in political science once told me:

I enjoy watching American movies. They are a lot of fun. Three or four years ago I used to be so involved in them that I hardly missed any with Paul Newman. I adore Paul Newman. He is the kind of man I imagine falling in love with. He is handsome, yet not quite attentive toward women. He is masculine and even rough sometimes. . . . The movie I really enjoyed was *Roman Holiday.* I saw it four times. Audrey Hepburn was so sweet, so nice. But I felt sorry for Gregory Peck. I almost felt if I were her, I would have left everything for him. How handsome and loving he was! Why is it that not a single young man in this city even comes close to his looks?

Girls in Calcutta have ample opportunity to see foreign movies (mostly from Hollywood) at least once a week if they can manage to find chaperones among their classmates and cousins. After seeing these movies, they continue talking among themselves about them for days on end.

Another area of idol-worship for a teen-aged girl is the cricket ground or tennis court. The glamour of cricket and tennis players is, of course, similar to the appeal a western movie star has for them. In the urban and semi-urban areas girls are often found discussing the kind of men they like. A man is considered handsome if he has a great element of physical smartness such as a cricket player displays. While these girls observe the *Śiva-rātrir brata* they also dream of a husband who will be a combination of Śiva, Krishna, Romeo, and Gregory Peck.

During her high school days, at the age of thirteen or fourteen, she has no male classmates, even though she may have quite a few male teachers. [29] They teach her English, Bengali, history (of India), geography (of the world), elementary science, and hygiene. She may also take elective courses in sewing and domestic science. Depending on the quality of the teaching, the charisma of the teachers, and the encouragement of her father who helps her with homework, she may develop a predilection for certain subjects. This may also depend on the available model she may have in one of her older siblings, but mostly because of her father's influence. This is also the time when she may decide to become a scientist, an economist, or even an engineer. In her schoolbooks she often comes across the names of great women scientists, women from both classical India and nineteenth-century Europe. Suddenly she sees the hope of liberation from the world of women—marriage, pregnancy, domineering mother-in-law—the world her female relatives are so carefully preparing her for. If she becomes a "famous" woman, she may escape all those things that, despite the intrigue that goes with them, create a kind of apprehension in her. Her apprehension comes because other women constantly emphasize the hardship of living in the husband's house and that pregnancy is the most painful experience a woman can have.

This occasional desire for liberation and consequent ambition comes about for two reasons. By the time she is twelve to thirteen years old, she notices that the future (*sasur-bāri*) that everybody constantly talks about does not necessarily promise endless bliss and happiness. At the same time, in spite of all the complaints and the grumbling that the women do about their *sasur-bāri*, they seem to enjoy it. She has to admit that the possibility of becoming like *choto kākimā* (the youngest aunt) with her newly married look and saris and jewelry, intrigues her; the possibility of becoming like her mother, with a husband like her father, is alluring; the possibility of spending long afternoons in gossip attracts her. At the same time, when she reads books about the great people of the world, when she listens to her father talk about philosophy and poetry or economics, she feels a great inspiration to become like him or one of those extraordinary women about whom the books speak. Even though her father may not direct her, the inspiration and desire to be a great woman usually comes from a desire to please her father, whom she has always admired, loved, and respected. This notion is not clear in her mind, although she knows that the inspiration is kindled by the father or by a father figure. A teacher at school may also add to this source of inspiration.

Other subjects discussed frequently at school are "the facts of life." This information she rarely learns from anyone at home. There are always a number of older and precocious classmates who know all about such matters. She learns the biological facts about a woman's body, about her menstrual cycle, pregnancy, and the connection between sexual intercourse and pregnancy. This information, of course, does not come as clinical talk; rather it is contained in interesting and exciting stories and pieces of gossip. She finds out that many of her friends accidentally have had opportunities to witness sexual acts. Someone may, for example, overhear the parents at night or be in the same room with a newly married couple; someone may have come across a pornographic magazine that her older brother had hidden under the mattress. Now she can guess the kind of "adult talk" her mother and younger aunts indulge in during some of the afternoon sessions. It has to do with "the facts of life."

Thus she learns about the physiology and sexual attitudes that go with adult life, and with marriage in particular. She begins to feel intrigued and excited about the whole thing; at the same time, it is clear to her that she is not supposed to feel excited and intrigued. She can tell from the amount of restrictions and taboos that are imposed on such talk at home and at school if adults happen to hear.

Case no. 12: I had a girl friend at school who was about four years older and came from another neighborhood where not many wealthy people lived. She used to tell me all about her parents' sexual relations. She also had an uncle, a cousin of her mother's, who lived with them. This uncle tried all sorts of undesirable things with her. At the beginning she was afraid and wanted to tell her mother, but the uncle threatened her that he would kill her if she told anybody. She was only eight at that time. Then gradually, she became used to his advances; she even liked it. She seemed to have lots of stories like that to tell me. Her uncle also gave her books full of dirty pictures; you know, the *battolā* types. [30] Some days she would bring them to school hidden inside her notebook and during the recess period we would go behind the hibiscus bushes at the edge of the playground to see those. We sat there talking about these things and kept an eye out in case the

game teacher found us or overheard us. I remember how I
enjoyed listening to these forbidden stories. It felt good to listen to
such things while we munched peanuts and *jhāl muri*. [31] The
other girls teased us because we always had so much to talk
about. They thought we had some secrets to share; so we did. It
was from her that I learned that the male thing looks different
from ours; and that the babies are not born by cutting the
stomach of the mother as my mother told me. She also told me
about menstruation—that all girls are destined to suffer every
month for a few days, and this has some connection with
marriage and having children. She asked me if I noticed anything
strange about my mother or aunts when they menstruate. They
are supposed not to put oil in their hair and not to enter the
kitchen. [32] I did not quite understand what she meant because I
never noticed my mother not entering the kitchen during any
particular time of the month. This piece of information about
menstruation came to me as a surprise and a piece of sad news. It
did not seem right to suffer like this, but I rationalized that
women are worse off than men in many respects. My mother
never told me these things. A couple of years later when I
menstruated myself, one of my older sisters explained to me how
to take care of the situation. But, no one said anything to reduce
my fear or depression about the matter.

From her peers she also learns about the connection between
romantic love and sex. She hears many stories, about a couple
eloping, about some young people found having intercourse
behind the walls of the hospital. She also hears things through her
siblings about young college students going to restaurants or
movies without telling their parents. She may see people kiss
inside a taxicab if she happens to be in a big city. By now it is
clear to her that one has to hide such behavior from older people
because one is not supposed to do this. Yet, one can do it when
married, even though nobody discusses or talks about it, except,
perhaps, young wives in their afternoon gossiping sessions.

Gradually she equates such knowledge with some of the stories
she has read in her schoolbooks and even some of the fairy tales,
told by her grandmother or others, that she listened to quite early
in her life. However, she is a bit confused as to whether this
prince and princess had the same kind of love as the couple
behind the hospital walls. Did they also do the things that

pornography illustrates? At the same time she is almost sure that the glow and flash she saw playing on *choto kākimā's* (father's younger brother's wife's) face when *choto kākā* (father's brother) entered the room suddenly has something to do with the "love" that all these stories, including the pornographic ones, talk about. It must also be the same thing when the movie stars sing in the moonlight, craving their beloveds. The love Behulā and Sitā had for their husbands must also mean the same thing. Why else would they go to all that trouble to save their husbands' life and honor? She is absolutely sure about Rādhā and Krishna, and of course, about Sakuntalā and Dyushmanta. And Romeo clearly talks about his love for Juliet. All these begin to connect with one another. She begins to feel love:[33] the romantic love that her childhood memories of fairy tales, stories, the poetry and classics that her father told her, the movies, and the occasional access to the pages of pornography brought to her in a blended mixture. She begins to wonder if she is going to love like Rādhā or like *choto kākimā*. One thing she is not clear about: Does her mother love her father the same way? Perhaps not. Does it mean then this kind of love does not exist in marriage? But then *choto kākā* and *choto kākimā* are married too; but Rādhā was not, nor was Juliet. Again, Sitā and Sāvitri were. At this stage she cannot resolve this particular problem, and she lets it rest for a while.

This newly acquired feeling and knowledge of love diverts her occasionally from her great resolution to become a great scientist. In her rush to taste the unknown bliss of romantic love as soon as possible, she begins to cherish the idea of marriage, the only acceptable way she can enter the world of love and happiness. She knows any other way is not proper. She would be very ashamed of herself if she had to go behind the hospital walls or into a park for this. She is also afraid that someone would find out and punish her. What would her father think of her? No, she has to wait like Śakuntalā for her husband to call her. This way she will not have to displease anybody. This realization of romantic love and hankering for it was expressed rather vividly by one informant who comes from a wealthy, westernized family.

Case no. 13: I was always very close to my father and his older brother. They took me out on trips to different places. I stayed in the convent at Kurseong, and father came to see me once every

month when he came to north Bengal on official business. Every
vacation father took the whole family to some nice place. Since I
stayed in a hill-resort to go to school, he preferred to go to a
sea-resort. He had a very close friend, an English doctor, who
also accompanied us most of the time. Dr. O'Malley had no wife
(nobody knew what happened to her); his only son Gregory came
with him, too. Gregory, like me, went to school somewhere in the
south and stayed in the hostel. I liked him very much. We saw
each other almost every Puja vacation and sometimes during
Easter also. I was thirteen that year when we all went to
Gopalpur and my mother did not come with us. It was just
father, me, Gregory, and his father. We stayed in a hotel. I think
I fell in love with Gregory during that vacation. I began to notice
how handsome he was. He had golden hair; his complexion was
like milk, and he was tall. His eyes were not blue though; they
were like mine. I thought he must look like a god, like the
descriptions one reads in a book. In fact, his features were so
delicate that he looked like the picture of Vishnu my mother had
in her room. I was so drawn to him that I began to imagine
myself as his wife. He often took a walk in the morning along the
driveway in front of the hotel, and I saw him from my window
and imagined myself by his side. From a distance he also looked
slightly older. I thought my father must have looked like him
when he was in England studying for his degree. It was silly to
think so. Because father had dark hair and he was shorter than
Gregory. All these thoughts I had about him; I never dared tell
anyone. When I came back to the convent again I lost interest in
everything. I could not concentrate on my studies. The only thing
I read was poetry and stories that talked about love. I knew I was
in love. I could not get over the idea that he looked like the
picture of Vishnu my mother had. He became my god, my
husband, and my lover in my dream. I waited for my father to
guess my condition and ask me if I would like to marry Gregory. I
knew that would never happen. But I kept hoping for it.

This is also the time when she reads novels both in Bengali
and English. Some of these books she is not allowed to read. Her
mother may have imposed a strong censorship on her reading,
because her mother feels that novels describing romantic love will
give her "ideas" before she is ready for them. She is around
fourteen or fifteen by now. She is also in the last class of her high
school. Soon she will be ready for marriage. The girl, however,

thinks in terms of possibly going to college. After she finishes her final exams she has three to four months of vacation before the results are announced. This is the time she reads a lot of English and Bengali novels. Authors such as Somerset Maugham, A. J. Cronin, Hemingway, and Jane Austen may be a major part of her reading, and in their novels romantic love plays an important role. Her mother does not impose any more restrictions because the daughter has crossed the boundary of high school. She is an adult now. She may have long discussions with her father or some of her older brothers and sisters about books and the characters therein. She also begins to go to foreign movies (if she happens to be in a big city) with her father or her peers.

This is also the time when she and her peers discuss "love" a great deal. The discussion is quite different from what she had at high school. Now they are not interested in gossip as such. They wonder about their future. They wonder if life and marriage will be like those they have been reading about in books and seeing in movies. She may indulge in dreams where her future husband will look like a famous cricket player or a movie star or one of the heroes of a novel.

Case no. 14: I used to sneak out to see the matinee shows of the English movies that the movie house in our town brought once every other week. I saw quite a few Hollywood pictures like this. Among us my friend Nina knew most about these movies; her English was also better than all of us. She got most of the conversation and explained it to us. When I first saw Gregory Peck I could not believe he could be so handsome. I asked Nina if I could get hold of a picture of his. She got me one from some foreign magazine. I had it hidden inside my blouse in a small case most of the time. At night before going to bed I would take it out and look and then sleep with the hope that I would dream of him. He would come to me and talk and perhaps kiss me the way he did that woman in the movie. While I was Gregory Peck's fan, Nina was Naresh Kumar's [the cricket player] and Sumita liked Uttam Kumar,[34] of course. We all had pictures of our idols and we constantly talked about them whenever we met. We also discussed the private lives of these people. I almost contemplated writing a letter to Gregory Peck to see what would happen. Something told us that if we were to be married soon, our

husbands would not be like them. We even discussed the
possibility of taking these pictures to our *sasur-bāri*. Sumita, who
was always more mature, said that that would be undesirable. It
is better to hope that at least one of our husbands will turn out to
be close to such idols.

   By now the father-daughter relationship develops into one of
companionship and friendship. She may even help him with his
work. If he is a schoolteacher or a college professor she may help
him with his grading of examinations. If he is a writer she may go
through his manuscripts and offer criticism. I knew of a
homeopath who taught his daughter how to diagnose illnesses
and prescribe medicine to some of his patients. She always helped
him and sometimes took care of his patients when he was not
around. She may also keep track of his finances and his correspondence. He begins to consult her on many matters when he
has to make a decision. His wife, who is too busy with other
children or household matters, accepts this quite naturally. This
is a phase that a girl becomes used to before she leaves the house
to become a college student or to be married. If not with her
father, she may become instead a close friend and companion to
an older brother. She may look after her father's physical
well-being. She may dictate his daily schedule of eating, sleeping,
and resting. She treats him almost like a child, as his mother did
and as his wife did at least for a short while soon after their
marriage. The daughter takes over the role of mother. The father
seems to enjoy it thoroughly. He leaves everything to her. This
dependence may reach a point at which the father may even take
his daughter with him on his business trips so that he does not
have to worry about small needs such as tea in the morning, milk
at night, or the crease of his trousers. [35]
   The mother's early resentment at the father's spending too
much time putting bookish ideas into the daughter's head is no
longer voiced, perhaps because it is the daughter who is spoiling
the father now. This seems quite acceptable to the mother as well
as to others in the family. In fact, the daughter is highly praised if
she looks after her father well. It is considered training, to learn
how to take care of an elderly man, because soon she will have to
care for her father-in-law.

Along with disciplining the younger girls the women in the house are also busy looking for possible matches for them. They leave the young girl alone for the time being, as if she has reached the stage when direct advice is unnecessary. There may be a few arguments between mother and daughter if the daughter talks about going to college. But the mother never takes such desires seriously, because she remembers arguing the same way with her own mother when she finished high school. She also remembers agreeing, rather eagerly, to be married when the proposal for marriage arrived. She knows that her daughter will forget such bookish ambitions when the time comes.

As for herself, the girl is beginning to become very self-conscious about her imminent role as wife. She is a bit confused about what she really wants. Somehow, all the burning ambitions she had throughout her school years look a bit less inviting. A change in manners and movement is obvious. She looks more mature and somber, and is perhaps a bit absent-minded. She listens to her mother and grandmother with a little more attention than she cared to pay them before. She looks at them with more sympathy. She begins to feel sad, thinking about the coming separation from her family. Suddenly she is no longer eager to escape the women's world. She feels she is one of them and is going to remain one of them. It may be a good idea to listen to them; after all, they have had the experience of marriage and life. She also feels ambivalent about her college studies, which the father talks about once in a while. They have to look into the admissions procedure if she is to make up her mind about which college to go to.

Case no. 15: During the three months after my final exams, I did a lot of reading. I divided up my day between reading and talking about the books with my father and chatting with my friends. I became my father's personal secretary. I kept track of his correspondence, his bank accounts. However, around this time I also grew a bit restless. I felt I should have enjoyed myself more. After long years of hard work at school at last I was free to enjoy a three-month vacation. Although my father and I always talked about the books I read, I also began to resent such serious talks for the first time. Some of my school friends seemed to spend more time chatting and gossiping, and I felt envious of them. I wanted to spend more time with my newly married aunt, for instance. They could tell me interesting things, I thought. I went shopping with my young aunt and cousins more frequently. They accepted me naturally, as if I were one of them, although my older sister occasionally taunted me by asking why I was not reading a heavy book instead. I enjoyed being with them and listening to their feminine talk. I wished I were married and had enough money and independence to buy my own saris and jewelry. Thought of marriage brought a tinge of sweet pleasure, as if everything would be changed for the better. Thought of a husband, who loomed somewhat vaguely in my daydream, intrigued me. Sometimes I got distracted, thinking of him while talking with my father. My father noticed such changes in me, and I felt embarrassed by my lack of attention and tried to avoid him for the next few days. As if someone was intruding between us. . . . Gradually, the idea of my going to a college did not appear as an alternative to marriage. There was no question in my mind that it would be nice to be married. That's what I wanted at that time very strongly. I visualized myself as a bride in all sorts of ways, in all the bright colors of saris and the best jewelry I could imagine. I even secretly put the end of my sari over my head and looked in the mirror to see how I would look when married. It became a routine pastime to indulge in these fantasies.

Her father and her brothers are a bit surprised at her sudden loss of enthusiasm for her studies. Perhaps they are even a bit disappointed. But, then, who can predict a woman's moods? [36] The women, especially the grandmother, watch this disappointment in the father and smile because they know this is the way a girl behaves when she is ready for marriage, her ultimate goal in life. It has always been this way, and is going to be forever.

A young upper-class or upper middle-class Bengali girl is given a very clear definition of her future role as a good wife and mother by the family and by society at large. This is done by direct verbal communication from the women often associated with disciplinary training; by exposing her to literary ideas and the characters of ideal women that have been read and talked about for generations; by exposing her to religious and household activities that women are properly engaged in; and by an attempt to restrict her association with the male world.

By the time a girl is twelve or thirteen, she knows exactly what is expected of her as a woman in marriage. The second kind of socialization comes primarily from the men in the family, her grandfather, father, uncles, and older brothers. Here she is exposed to less direct verbal advice as to her future expected role. She is treated with great tenderness and affection and importance. She learns to feel wanted and cared for. Along with this indulgence she is exposed to the academic and artistic sides of life. She listens to the reminiscences of her grandfather who stimulates her imagination and arouses fantasies within her. Later she is given famous classics to read. Unlike her female relatives, the men do not select particular themes only. Her school work, which has little to do with her everyday life, becomes an intellectual enterprise, and her father reinforces it by helping her. He makes it clear that there is great value in reading and learning for its own sake. She learns to enjoy it not merely intellectually but emotionally because the subject matter of many of these books appeals to her growing imagination. Besides, she associates this category of learning with the male figures she loves and admires—her father, uncles, and possibly a male teacher. She is even inspired to escape into this world of intellect and imagination, away from the practical world of women with all its anticipation of hardship in the *sasur-bāri*.

There is a third source outside the family that reinforces the internalization and synthesis of these first two levels. The women's world often gives her messages, not conscious or overt, that may go beyond dry advice about how to become a good wife and mother. By observing women dress, by listening to them talk, and by observing them reacting to men, a girl picks up cues and discovers that there are possibilities of escape even within the set framework of the hard rules that a married woman is expected to follow.

An additional source of reinforcement in the process of synthesis comes from her peers at school and in the neighborhood, the readings that are forbidden to her, the movies that she sees occasionally, and the exchanges that she has with her friends (that she cannot have with anyone in the family including brothers and sisters). All these combine to give her a particular kind of experience, which makes her aware of such facts as the sexual component of an adult life. Given her social and familial background, this is a realm that is forbidden to her in both direct and indirect experience. It is all very intriguing to her.

On the level of synthesis she thus has three kinds of information and knowledge. The first is important for her to internalize, the second is what she may indulge in, and the third is what she wants to know, but which is forbidden to her.

When she is fifteen or sixteen and has finished her high school education, the connection between the three levels is still not clear to her. She hopes that life, married life, will provide her the opportunity to realize all three. She has developed into a young woman. Physically and psychologically, her natural tendencies are to find ways to realize and express herself as a woman. The only acceptable and commendable way provided by society is marriage. Marriage, therefore, becomes something to look forward to. It presents more mystery and hope than anything else.

There do not seem to be any alternatives left for the girl. Even though her male relatives do not constantly talk about her going to *sasur-bāri*, as her women relatives do, still they take it for granted that this is her future. In fact, the affective content of the close father-daughter relationship becomes intense because it is understood that she will be "going away." Her peers, who do not belong to either of the two worlds in her family, also seem to know of no other alternatives. Marriage is her destiny. She can only hope for the best. She brushes off the unresolved problem of the apparent lack of connection between the ideal wife-mother figure and the romantic lover-consort figure outside marriage that she reads so much about. She prepares herself to take the plunge and hopes that her husband may turn out to be a combination of her father, her male teachers, the characters in novels, movies, and plays, and cricket players, even though watching her mother and father does not give her any indication that these hopes will be realized. On the other hand, her newly married aunt (the *choto kākimā*) and her young uncle (*choto kākā*) seem to suggest something qualitatively different from the relationships her parents and the older couples in the family have. This is a question, a puzzle, and the answer must be sought in marriage.

3 Marriage

Preparation for the Marriage

Negotiation. In a joint upper-class Bengali home when a girl finishes her high school she has two alternatives open to her. One is to be married within six months or a year; the other is a college education, with the anticipation that by the end of the second or third year of college she will be married. If there is no good match available by then she will go through another year or two of college and in most cases she is married by the time she earns her bachelor's degree. These four years are actually a transition period in which she prepares herself for marriage while her family finds her a good match. From the point of view of her family, she may as well spend the time going to college to keep herself busy while she is waiting for a good match to be negotiated. The family that accepts her going to college for this interim period is likely to be less conservative than others and may feel that extra education will not interfere with her married life. One added rationale for allowing her four years of college is that by acquiring a B.A. degree she adds to her credentials for a better marriage. For example, a family with an eligible bachelor who holds foreign degrees or works in a foreign firm may require a couple of college degrees as part of the girl's qualifications, because their son obviously needs a wife who will be able to speak English and be intelligent enough to socialize with his office colleagues. Also, if she has a B.A. or BSc. degree, his family may even settle for a smaller dowry.

Whether a girl goes on to higher education after graduating from high school also depends on her high school results, the financial condition of the family, the availability of a college near the family home, and so on. Above all, she must have strong backing from her male relatives, who can convince the women that all this is worthwhile. Besides, the family may need time to raise the cash for the wedding expenses and dowry, and to find a good match.

Whether the girl is going to college or not, she knows that sooner or later she has to be ready for marriage. She is expected to learn a few cooking recipes, and to do a little sewing such as embroidering tablecloths and pillowcases. If she excels in these endeavors, a few pieces may be saved to be included in her dowry. She also continues to read both Bengali and English novels and continues to spend time with her peers in chats, movies, and shopping. Her freedom of movement is somewhat greater now. She can go shopping or have coffee at the coffee houses in town with her classmates or cousins who live in the house, provided she keeps certain hours. Since she is not usually encouraged to go to a coeducational college, her peer group still consists of girls alone. Her cousins and classificatory brothers may also accompany her to certain places and spend relatively more time with her than they did when she was younger.

This gives her opportunities to develop affectionate and friendly relationships with her male cousins and brothers, the only young males she is exposed to. She begins to realize the charm of spending time with young men who pay attention to her looks and clothes and tease her about her studies and future marriage. This association, in other words, makes her aware of her feminine appeal to men. This is the time when she learns to feel very much at home with the younger male relatives who provide her with companionship, friendship, and subtle flattery. She likes the feeling of being a woman in the company of these men.

The women in the house, especially the older ones, devote themselves totally to the search for a good marriage match. Typically, they conduct the hunt on their own by writing to distant relatives for information on marriageable bachelors and their families. These families, having similar economic and cultural backgrounds, are from the same caste, but not necessarily the same subcaste. The use of newspaper advertisements and professional matchmakers may also bring a number of possibilities to their attention. Two other people are important in this connection. A widowed elderly aunt (e.g., a father's sister living with the family) may become one of the main leaders in the hunt. Women of her kind, without familes of their own, are considered the right persons for this. She may be helped by an elderly maid who has been with the family for a number of years or perhaps has attended the girl as a baby. Old maidservants are considered particularly qualified for this because they happen to be well-versed in the inner workings of neighborhood families. Thus, in the initial stage, the whole business of groom-hunting goes on in the women's world. Once the possibilities look optimistic, the grandmother may consult the older males in the household, the grandfather and the older uncles. The father is not consulted for the time being if his older brothers are around.

At this stage many families exchange the horoscopes of the prospective bride and groom to see if they match. This is done through the mail unless the families live in the same city. If the horoscopes indicate serious difficulties toward a marriage match, some orthodox families may terminate the negotiation at this stage. In case of minor discord, a few conciliatory offerings to particular stars may be made in the form of religious rites.

It seems that horoscopes are not considered seriously if the rest of the conditions are well-matched. There are some families in urban Bengal where horoscopes are not even consulted, sometimes because the young people may not have one cast because the families do not place importance on such traditional customs.

The groom these families look for should meet the standard idea of a good man: one who has a high college degree (preferably in medicine or engineering), a respectable family background (with educated men in good government jobs), and a good job, preferably with a high salary. He may be between five and ten years older than the girl and he should be in good health. His complexion (which is very important in a girl's case) and features are not considered significant.

At the second stage of marriage negotiation, the girl is told by one of her older female siblings or sisters-in-law that the proposal is advancing and very soon the boy's family may come to see her. Although this is quite an acceptable custom in other classes of Bengal and most of India, the expression "to see the bride" (*kone dekhā*) immediately creates mixed resentment in an upper-class Bengali girl. She cannot bring herself to the idea of being "inspected" and "watched" as a market commodity. She argues with her mother and grandmother and complains to her father. She may try to coax her grandfather to let her out of it. She resents it so strongly because she knows that her lower-class counterpart is subjected several times to such humiliation before she is married off. What difference exists then, she asks, between someone like her with education and a better family background and a lower-class girl? The idea hurts her sense of self and her dignity. She may be able to mobilize her cousins and younger sisters-in-law who see the point easily and in turn mobilize the opinion of the older people. The point that this girl, who comes from a better family, should undergo such a humiliating inter-view appeals to the older people more than anything else. The family may be talked into arranging something more acceptable to the younger people.

One acceptable method is a trip to a movie or a restaurant where the boy is introduced to the girl in the presence of his friends and her married sisters and perhaps a brother. The latter act as chaperones and do most of the talking. In a movie, there is hardly any chance to talk. Coffee afterwards in a restaurant may allow the group to talk about small things—her studies, his interest in soccer games, and so on. It's the boy's friends who do most of the talking to the girl's chaperones, and questions are put indirectly and with an overtone of joking and humor. Thus it does not appear as if she is being interviewed by the boy's friends, even though the parties are aware of the businesslike quality of the encounter. A typical encounter like this may be represented by the following case.

Case no. 16: I had been hearing a lot about this particular proposal. My younger sister brought me bits and pieces of information that she overheard while my mother and the aunts were discussing it. I learned from my sister, for example, that his family was wealthy and he had finished his engineering degree. He was twenty-seven and, according to my sister who saw the photograph, quite handsome. My sister offered to steal the photograph from my uncle's desk if I were curious to have a look. Of course I was curious. But I felt a bit shy to tell her that, yet I did not want to let the opportunity slip by. So I told her and made her promise not to tell anybody that I asked her to do so. We felt excited about the complicity. When she succeeded in stealing it out of the desk drawer for a few minutes I could not tell if I really liked his looks. My sister told me she saw several other apparently discarded photographs in the desk. The picture looked like any other young man: I tried to search within myself some sort of feeling for this man whose face I saw on a piece of paper. Then one day *mejo-boudi* [the wife of the middle brother] told me that we were going to have tea with a group of young men in the "Kwality" restaurant and I should take a nap so that I would look presentable. My sister gave me the rest of the information that he and his friends were coming to the restaurant to "see" me. That Sunday I washed my hair, took a long bath, and felt as if something important was going to happen to me. I felt happy and tense. In the afternoon, *boudi* [sister-in-law], *sejdi* [third older sister], and *dādā* [older brother] and I took a taxi to the Kwality restaurant on Park Street. A group of four men were sitting at a table already. The inside of the restaurant was cool and darker than outside. *Dādā* led us to the table and for a split second my eyes met the eyes of the face I saw in the picture. He looked better than in the photograph. We all sat down. I did not raise my head lest I catch his eyes again. I could feel all the other eyes on me. They began to talk while I was stirring my tea self-consciously. One of his friends suddenly asked me if I intended to finish my B.A. and whether I read any poetry. When I looked up to answer my eyes again met his; he was watching me. I felt rather nervous and mumbled that I would like to finish my degree and I read poetry occasionally. Before I finished, my sister-in-law interrupted with a smile and asked the friend, "Does your friend read poetry? If that's where his interests lie, we will see to it that our girl has all the poetry books on her bedside table." Everybody smiled at that. *He* looked down, and another friend asked me if I enjoyed cooking. While I nodded mildly (because I seldom got a chance to cook), my sister-in-law said,

"Oh, yes, she sings when she stirs her curry." Everybody laughed at that. After that the men began to talk about the latest soccer game while *dādā* asked *him* about his office, his work, and his future plans, carefully avoiding the question of salary. I sat there sipping cold tea and half-listening and half-wondering if I could love this man if I were to be married to him. Suddenly *he* asked me if I would like another cup of hot tea and before I replied he called the waiter. I was quite impressed by his attention. I thought he had a deep voice; I felt closer to him.

While coming home *boudi* asked me jokingly if I liked him. I did not say anything and looked away. After a month my sister ran to me one morning to announce that I was to be married next month to the same man. The proposal had been made. I felt a sharp tinge of happiness and tried to remember the face of the man who offered a hot cup of tea to me in the restaurant.

From this, and from many similar descriptions, it is clear that the girl has no opportunity to meet the boy alone before the wedding ceremony is over. All they can know about each other is the impression they get from a short chaperoned encounter that takes place in an artificial setting. This recent custom seems to have been designed to give lip-service to the demand that people should meet before they are married. Typically the girl is chaperoned to such meetings only when the marriage proposal is well advanced and the chances of breaking up the negotiation is minimal. There may be situations where a girl has been to two or three such meetings before one negotiation is completed. In some families, if the older generation happens to be particularly conservative, they may not allow her to go out to such encounters. Instead she is "seen" formally in her house by the father and other male relatives of the boy. The setting is equally contrived and even more formal. Women are always excluded from this meeting, except one sister-in-law who may accompany the girl to the sitting room where the guests are waiting. She serves tea and snacks to the guest and is asked to sit down. The men who came to look her over begin to ask a number of questions along the following lines:

Do you know how to cook *sukto*?
Have you read *The Mahābhārata, The Rāmayana*?

Which story of *The Mahābhārata* do you like best? Why?
Can you sing a *bhajan* [devotional song] for us?

The major part of the interview is, however, the careful observation of the girl and her family by the men of the boy's family. They look for good omens [1] in her person and carriage. They also note if she has been spoiled by western college education or if she is still very quiet, subdued, and docile. It is important for her to show signs of obedience and docility if she is to make a good wife and daughter-in-law. It is also important because she will have to live with other women under the same roof. If she shows indications of independence and arrogance, the kind of attitudes modern girls tend to pick up in college, she will definitely not make a good daughter-in-law. The future groom may himself be part of the group of inspectors, but he hardly opens his mouth and the girl hardly dares to look up to see what he looks like. The situation can be quite embarrassing for the boy if he happens to have some of the modern ideas his older male relatives are so afraid of. [2]

For these interviews the girl is made to dress up in her best sari and finery in order to highlight her looks and other qualities. Her mother and grandmother tell her time and again that she should keep her eyes downcast all the time she is in the company of those respected men. She should join her palms gracefully while greeting them and talk in a low voice and only in very short sentences when asked a question. They also make her practice a devotional song or two, the kind older people are supposed to like. The point that is emphasized is the modesty and grace of her manners and movements, because according to Bengali standards these are the most desirable qualities in a bride.

The belief that certain qualities in a girl are symptomatic of her potential success as a wife and mother, and the expectations accompanying this belief, is so deep-seated that no one questions its validity. Whether a half-hour interview is enough to indicate such crucial symptoms is another question no one regards as relevant. In fact, the potential groom's family already has some preliminary information on the girl's manners and conduct from indirect sources. In Bengali society, if a girl is not well-behaved the neighbors talk about it and the matchmakers do not have to dig too far to get such facts. In other words, the girl must know what is expected of her if she is to be a good daughter-in-law and wife and mother. In a girl who is allowed to be chaperoned to the movie or the restaurant to meet her future husband and his friends a kind of romantic expectation about him arises. The fact that she can meet her future husband before the night of the wedding makes her feel important. It is as if a bond is already established between them. This, however, is usually nothing but fantasy on her part, which is fed by her reading and the other information that go along with marriage. At the same time, it helps her to dream about him and prepare herself to accept him as her future husband. She has now a concrete image of a husband and she begins to imagine things about him. Meanwhile, her family supplies food to her imagination by discussions of the boy's family, talk of the measurement of his wedding shirt or her ring finger, and so on. Her sisters and cousins tease her constantly, and all seem to enjoy this teasing enormously. All this may lead the girl to live in a constant fantasy, and she easily works up a lot of feeling and emotion for her husband-lover whom she will meet very soon as Rādhā met Krishna.

Case no. 17: After I met my future husband briefly, when all of us went to a movie, I kept thinking about him constantly. While watching the movie I identified myself with the heroine and wondered what was going on in his mind. There were at least five people between us, so I could not even see his face. I thought he was very handsome. Something told me he was the one I would marry. It was just a feeling; like fate, you know. It never occurred to me for a moment that it might not happen. After a month or so, when I heard that the proposal was final and I was to be married within three weeks, my days and nights were nothing but a dream full of him. I am sure I imagined more than he really was. He soon took the shape of the ideal man I had been waiting for, I always wanted to marry. Now after twelve years of married life this sounds more than ridiculous. It's hard to believe that I was that stupid. Anyway, I kept thinking about him all the time and began to neglect my studies and everything including my friends. I behaved as if I was sleepwalking or dazed all the time. Suddenly I saw no point in getting a B.A. degree any more. Yet I wanted to be a college professor. My friends began to tease me because I was showing all the symptoms of a girl in love. And

I was in love. I worked up so much feeling for this unknown husband of mine that I began to write love letters to him and hid them under my pillow. I had to express all my feelings for him; then one day I became very bold and sent him a letter. I got hold of his office address somehow. I poured my heart out in that letter. But as soon as I dropped it in the mail I became scared. Suppose he disliked my immodesty. Then for over a week I was extremely nervous anticipating a scolding letter from him. I even imagined that he would break the proposal because I was so shameless to do such a thing. It was not done. I was also afriad that his letter might fall in someone's hands and the whole thing would be out and I would be punished. Anyway, his letter never arrived. I was relieved thinking that he never got it. Later, after I had been married several weeks, I asked my husband if he ever received a letter from me. He said no. That relieved me. Perhaps it really got lost or perhaps I wrote the address wrong. Now after all these years of married life, knowing my husband quite well, I suspect he got the letter all right but did not know what to do with it. I must have shocked him by my silly romanticism and the shamelessness I showed in expressing it.

Thus psychologically the girl is quite prepared to be married without any question about the plausibility of her romantic expectations. About the rights and duties of a married woman she has some theoretical knowledge, but nobody explicitly talks about relations between husband and wife. At any rate, she is not worried about that right now. She is very much involved with her ideas about a man she is in love with, someone she will love and from whom she expects to receive love in return. This does not depend on any particular romantic overtures from the man. Nor does he have to look like a movie star for that. He embodies the idea of a husband and that is enough to trigger such expectations. This buildup of romantic expectations about the marriage, and about the husband in particular, is also important for her as a defense against all the uncertainty and fear she has about the sasur-bāri (father-in-law's house).

The question of her rejecting the man at this stage of negotiation may come up only if through such short encounters she gets a very strong negative impression of him, accompanied by some dubious information, that he may be having an affair with the widow next door or is addicted to gambling or alcohol or some such thing. But the chances of her having access to such information without the knowledge of the family are very slim. Should this happen, she may indicate her feelings to one of her older sisters or brothers or her sisters-in-law, who may transmit it to the older relatives. If it is just a question of her "impression" they brush such objections aside and make her understand the futility of "such impressions" in marriage. The women may talk to her at great length, for example, about the irrelevance of thinking that good looks on the part of the husband will insure a good marriage, until she gives in. If the girl's objection is based on some facts about his personal life, they may investigate and cancel the proposal if the information turns out to be true.

As for the man, he has more freedom to cancel a proposal if he finds objections regarding the girl. In his case the short encounters may be decisive, since a girl's looks and appearance are considered of more significance. If he dislikes the way she looks he may legitimately reject her without offering any other reasons. His family accepts such objections without much ado because in the marriage market a man is more in demand than is a girl. They know that finding another suitable bride may not be difficult. As a male, earning member of the joint-family, he has more say in his family than a marriageable girl has in hers.

The Wedding. When the wedding date is set after consultation with a priest, the preparations begin in earnest. The priest may consult an almanac to determine the most auspicious time for the wedding to take place. There are some months in which a person born under a certain zodiac sign cannot be married because the result may be such a disaster as widowhood. All families, including the urban upper class, believe in this procedure before the marriage of their children. The women busy themselves shopping for saris, household materials, linens, kitchenwares, furniture. Jewelers will visit regularly in the afternoons with their huge catalogs waiting to take orders. The girl will be consulted in choosing the pattern of her necklaces and bangles and so on. She is also encouraged to join the women in shopping sprees when her personal dowry is being purchased. She may be allowed to choose her saris, the furniture, and the design of the brass dishes as well. She enjoys all this very much. She may skip her classes at college to join her sisters-in-law for shopping trips. Besides being interested in possessing nice things, she also enjoys her sudden change of status. She has become the center of everything. All the activities in the household are revolving around her and her wedding. The whole household is planning and spending money, time, and energy on her. The men are busy drawing up lists of guests and arranging the construction of a tent for the seating of all the guests, or discussing whether the hiring of the school building would be better. They also keep corresponding with the groom's family on essential matters such as the transaction of dowry, the transportation of the groom and his retinue, and so on.

A couple of days before the wedding, the prologue of the ceremony begins. Women get busy in various feminine rites[3] that are symbolic for the girl. For example, a ceremonial bath in Ganges water (or the equivalent if the place is far from the river) several times a day is supposed to purify her body and soul. The women sing a kind of wedding song to accompany these baths. The lyrics of the songs strongly emphasize the importance of the coming event in the girl's life. Some of the songs harp on the theme of the earthy and crude facts of married life: how to attract the husband's attention by looking voluptuous and so on. Some weave the theme of the sorrow of her leaving her natal family, and some tell her about the hardship of *sasur-bāri*.

I do not have many examples of the songs sung by the older ladies during a wedding. A few are given below.

> By pouring fried rice on the *kodā* [a bird],
> Let me be wife of a king.
> By pouring sugar on the head of the *kodā*,
> Let me be a queen,
> By pouring *ghee* on the head of the *kodā*,
> Let me be the daughter of the king.

> Oh Hara! I pray to thee for a boon,
> Let my husband be a king.
> And let my cowife be a maid,
> And once a year let me come to my father's house.

> Temple with the *banglas* [bungalows],
> Elephants at the door and the horses outside,

Servants and maids, cows and buffaloes,
Wander here and near.
[With] youth and beauty [I am] always happy,
[And] my husband loves me.

[Collected and translated by Geeti Sen, University of
Chicago; personal correspondence.]

Both the melody and the words are very touching. Because of
this, the girl's emotions reach a higher state of mixed pleasure,
sorrow, and importance. Since most of these songs, which
continue to be sung by hired professional women (or some older
relatives who have little to do), emphasize the pathos of her
imminent separation from her beloved family, the girl feels the
tragedy of a woman's life. For a while she moves from the world
of her imagined romantic world of love to the apprehension of
losing another kind of love, her father's and siblings' and mother's
love. This is so dramatized that it becomes difficult for her not to
feel very sad. The only way she can cope with it is by hoping that
her future with her husband will make her forget this sorrow. She
hopes that she will find the same kind of love and affection in her
new household.

In this ceremonial atmosphere of which the girl is the center,
all the women strongly press the point of her departure and the
seriousness of the ceremony. She is lifted into a special status for a
few days till the actual wedding night arrives. All these days she
has been separated from her male relatives. She avoids her father
particularly, because she cannot stand seeing him so depressed
and so tired. He is not only too busy with the arrangement of the
ceremony, but he also looks sad because of his beloved daughter's
imminent departure. She is no longer a daughter or a niece or a
granddaughter, but a bride—a very special status. During the
wedding ceremony, which takes several hours, the most significant part is "the giving away" (*dān*) by the father or one of the
father-figures. The bride, along with the dowry, is given away to
the groom in front of the god of fire who, according to the Vedic
scriptures, acts as the only witness of a Hindu wedding. This
particular rite is of tremendous significance to all three people—
the bride, the father, and the bridegroom. The bride is dressed in
her bridal sari with all her jewelry and, watched by hundreds of

eyes, sits in front of a smoking sandalwood fire repeating the Sanskrit verses after the priest. Her father (the mother is not allowed to watch the wedding) puts her right palm on the groom's right palm and ties them together with a white flower garland; she sits cross-legged, feeling the touch of the hand of the man she hopes to love all her life. This, combined with the smoke, music, the presence of people, the Sanskrit verses, and the fact that she has fasted all day to purify the body and soul (as have both her father and husband), makes her feel dazed and nearly dizzy. A Hindu girl has been socialized to marry an unknown man in such a religious ceremony, and in the ceremony she easily transcends her surroundings and makes believe that she has a special status as a responsible wife, with all its solemn, religious association. Take the following confession from a college graduate.

Case no. 18: I still remember the wedding night. I must admit something very special happens when you sit there in the presence of all these people and music and flowers and everything else. I almost believed that it was the best thing that ever happened to me. My husband to whom I was just wedded held my hand very gently and I felt I knew this touch. The look of my father, reciting the *mantras* after the priest, gave me the sad feeling that he really was giving me away. I broke down with sobs; someone from the crowd came and held me and wiped my eyes. I do not think I cried because I was particularly sad, but I felt very emotional and light as if nothing mattered anymore. I was also very tired from the whole day's ceremony and fasting, I guess. This was a feeling, I suppose, no woman ever feels again.

Thus during the ceremony the bride enters a near-trance state, generated by the conflicting emotional tension between the sorrow of leaving her family and the excitement of becoming the wife of a young man and going to live with his family. The wedding scene seems to have been designed to intensify the emotional tension in her. There is another part of the ceremony that is of particular significance. In Bengal, among the Hindus of the upper class, "the exchange of garlands" takes place before the "giving away." The exchange of garlands is almost an equivalent of the exchange of rings in a Christian wedding. The bridegroom sits on a decorated chair while the bride is carried on a wooden seat by her brothers around the bridegroom seven times (or she may walk). After every round she stops in front of him, bows her head in the fashion of greeting, and offers flowers and colored powder such as worshipers offer to the deity in a temple. The colored powder is used for the Holi festival with the implication that the god Krishna played with his gopinis (the cow-girls that he flirted with) with such colored powder. At any rate, the bride goes through her seven rounds and at the end exchanges her flower garland with the bridegroom's flower garland. She is also supposed to "look" at him for the first time. A piece of silk material covers their heads and they look at each other ceremoniously. During this particular part of the wedding, the girl invokes her deity, the husband, with the same kind of material (flowers) worshipers use for deities in the temples; she finds it hard not to think of the man sitting on the chair as anyone but her god, a very personal one. Her romantic expectations, all the imaginative speculation she has indulged in up to this point, take on the color of a religious devotion. She identifies herself with Rādhā whose god and lover she has so intensely craved for. Then follows the "giving away" ceremony; it is not hard to understand why the bride may find the ceremony an intensely emotional event.

While the Hindu wedding emphasizes rites symbolizing devotion toward the husband-god, it also includes a series of rites that symbolize the physical closeness between the married partners. During the ceremony, the bridegroom has to hold the bride's hand several times, put his arms around her while they jointly offer flowers to the god of fire, and, at other times feed her sweets. All these rites are supposed to bring them physically closer, so that the bride gradually becomes used to his touch. The couple is discouraged from consummating the marriage the first night, even though they share the same bed. The custom of peeping into the bridal chamber prevents the couple from indulging in any physical closeness. This peeping, done by the female relatives, may be so annoying that the couple, after such a grueling and tense day, is not allowed to rest. Usually the middle-aged women enjoy this particular sport and go to any length to reach the skylight or the bathroom door. Some of them even pretend to be men and hide under the bed and start giggling and wriggling as soon as the couple makes any movement. The rest of the wedding night continues to be filled with women running, giggling, and whispering around the bridal room. This custom of peeping into the bridal chamber appears to have been designed to make the wedding night a public scene, to give the couple some breathing space, as it were, before they become sexually involved.

Let me go back to the feelings of the bridegroom during the wedding. Most men find it hard to recall their exact feelings as well as the women can. They all know about the emotional stress a woman endures; they sympathize with it. They feel rather self-conscious at being placed in a position where the audience pays curious attention. The bridegroom, who is treated like a royal guest and sits in the middle in his specially made wedding attire, feels little of anything. He wishes the whole busines to be soon over. He is simply tired and exhausted from fasting and traveling perhaps (many bridegrooms do not fast today). To him, all the customs and rites are either silly or the usual things that one has to put up with in life. His grandfathers and father and uncles all had to go through it; and it's no use rebelling against such things because women usually have their way. He might as well go through it and take the bride home and begin married life. He is usually accompanied by a group of friends or cousins who keep teasing him about the future possibilities, mostly of a sexual kind. The religious and aesthetic content of the ceremony, which creates so much emotion in his bride, somehow has little impact upon him. He takes it as a matter-of-fact procedure necessary to acquire a wife. During the ceremony of "giving away" the only emotion he goes through is the slight feeling of responsibility that this particular act symbolizes. He is going to be the husband of this beautiful bundle of sari and jewelry, and society, including her tired-looking father, expects him to look after her. Other than that, he hardly feels any great emotion about anything. He may feel a bit embarrassed and self-conscious about being so important for the whole evening. But the presence of his friends, who are constantly engaged in jokes and fun and mild flirting with other girls, brings back his natural status of a man who is only going through a day of ceremony to obtain a wife, as the following confession by a man illustrates.

Case no. 19: I do not particularly remember anything except the usual fatigue and exhaustion of the endless rituals. I almost felt sorry for the bride because she had to go through even more. During the *dān* I recall clearly how my eyes burned because of the damn fire-smoke they call god. I was also very hungry from the long travel. All I wanted was a bed to lie down in; but those women never left us alone till the next morning. I almost lost my temper when they began to bother us in the bedroom. While leaving my wife's house the next day I felt a bit sad when I saw her sob so profusely, and all the women in the household weeping for her. But then all girls weep when they go to their *sasur-bāri* and also forget it very soon. All they need is *bier jal*[4] to forget everything. I felt almost like a villain in a Bombay movie, as if I were snatching away the daughter of the house. But this feeling lasted only a few minutes till we left the town.... I tell you, the wedding itself has very little significance for us, the men. It is one of those things one has to go through in life.

The second day after the wedding is usually spent in travel to the bridegroom's house. If the two families live close by, the wedding party may not leave until the day after. The bride sleeps with her mother the second night, which is considered her last night in her father's home. She also needs a night's rest after the strain of the days before. The last phase of the wedding is the ceremonial departure of the bride and her husband from her father's home. This phase is very tense and charged with emotion. Her female relatives weep profusely. Her father, who looks worn out from the strain of the responsibility of the wedding ceremony, also looks very sad. He avoids any direct contact with his daughter lest he break down completely. He may be found hidden in the corner of his study or on the roof hiding his tears. He looks after the organizational details to the very end of the ceremony with a heavy heart. The grief and sorrow of the separation from his daughter is so intense that the only way he can transcend it is by reminding himself of the harsh "way of life," the duties a father must accept. He remembers how the father of the goddess Durgā (Umā) gave her away to her husband Śiva and how the whole kingdom grieved for her. But the father had to tolerate this separation. He also remembers the great sage Kanya in Kālidāsa's *Śakuntalā* and his laments when his beloved daughter Śakuntalā had to leave his āshram to meet her husband

Dyushyanta. These examples from the classics and scriptures make him feel better and he can lift himself onto a plane where he becomes a sacrificing father for the good of his daughter. This is his only consolation. As a good father and upright member of society he has to go through this role, no matter how painful.

Case no. 20: When I left my father's home the day after my wedding, I was very sad. I could not bear to look at my father's face, which was thin and emaciated from fasting the day before [if the father performs the ceremony of *dān* he also has to fast along with the couple]. I avoided him the whole day till the time came to leave when I touched my head to his feet. He raised me with his hands and kissed me on my head and embraced me very tenderly. Our tears mingled. That very moment I felt I could not leave him; I could not leave such security and affection for something so unknown. How shall I be able to accept another man as my father? How shall I be able to call him father when my own father is the only one I know as my father? After I left, during the train trip to my husband's town, I constantly thought of my father and also the others in the family. A week after I reached my *sasur-bāri* I received a very nice letter from my father. He wrote out the whole verse from Kālidāsa's *Śakuntalā* where the sage Kanya was having a monologue with himself when Śakuntalā was leaving him to join her husband. He mentioned at the end of the letter briefly that I must do my duties as a good wife and a daughter-in-law. He could only console himself if I became a good daughter to my father-in-law, my new father. He would be very proud of me. He also sent a couple of books that I used to read and liked. The letter made me cry again.

The third night after the wedding is the ritual night of consummation. This is called the night of "flower bed." This is actually the first night at the husband's house, and the bed is decorated with the flowers of the season. There is a short ceremony before the couple enters the bedroom. Before that, when the new couple enters the premises of the *sasur-bāri*, the mother-in-law welcomes them ceremonially. A few small rites are worth mentioning here. The daughter-in-law is given honey to taste and a drop of honey is put into her two ears, indicating that she should always speak sweetly and hear sweet things in this household. Sometimes, a pot of milk is boiled in the kitchen and allowed to overflow as soon as she crosses the threshold to symbolize the wish that her entry to the family may cause an overflow of fortune.

Every young man and woman has a lot of romantic expectations about the "flower bed" evening. The men have been hearing all sorts of stories and jokes about this night. They hear detailed descriptions from their friends and their friends' friends. They also read lots of stories based on the experience of this night. These stories emphasize the excitement of a sexual experience with a wife who is not only a virgin and inexperienced, but also very romantic, full of love, and eager to give herself. For many men in this society, the night may also offer their first sexual experience. While they prepare themselves all these years to conquer the woman they are given to enjoy, their preparation lacks the strong romantic element their wives have. This is not because they do not read or hear the romantic literature about this evening or about marriage in general, but because most of what they learn from their friends and reading gives a very crude picture of the first sexual union of the couple. This is also deeply rooted in the attitude men in Indian culture, and in Bengal in particular, have been nurturing for centuries. Be that as it may, the husband's expectations definitely differ from those of the wife. For him it is also the first time (in most cases) that he is given a socially acceptable opportunity to prove his sexual worth by manipulating all sorts of strategies in the game of sex to coax his bride to yield. He has been told by his friends that usually the brides are eager to give in even though they pretend to be shy and modest. It intrigues him to find out about his particular bride and he looks forward to relating the story to his friends the next day. Consider the following narrative by a young man.

Case no. 21: After my cousin, who was close to my age, got married, we eagerly waited to get him to talk about his sexual experiences with his bride. He used to come and join the group of friends at the corner teashop where six of us sat every Sunday morning and chatted and gossiped about girls mostly. All men do that, as you know. This particular teashop is very popular for that purpose since it is located at the major intersection of roads leading to the shopping areas, music schools, and parks. All you have to do is stand at the corner for five minutes and at least the ten most beautiful girls of South Calcutta [the residential part of the city] will walk by. You can even smell their expensive perfume. Anyway, our gang makes sure that we get there before the place is crowded. The table we usually occupy has an added advantage of being next to the window looking over one of the main streets. So we can stare at girls, sip our tea, and talk about sex at the same time. I tell you, these Sunday mornings are the only thing in my life I look forward to, the rest of the week.... Oh, going back to my cousin, he could not come the first Sunday after his wedding. We were highly disappointed. Next Sunday, I dragged him out of his home and brought him to the teashop. We had dozens of questions for him. At first he blushed a little, then he told us how it all happened. How his bride first put up some resistance and how later loved *it* and now hardly leaves him alone every night. After we really kept insisting on the details he even told us about the size and shape of various parts of her body. He confessed hers did not look like some of the pictures in the books we all shared and looked at and that disappointed him a bit at the beginning.

Since then every Sunday for about a couple of months the first thing he would tell us was the number of times he and his wife had had intercourse the week before. We all enjoyed listening to it till it became a drag and we dropped the topic of my cousin's marriage and went back to our girl-watching, waiting for someone else to get married.

The idea of owning a young, beautiful woman, sexually and emotionally, also intrigues the husband. He knows that from now on he can depend on a woman's total attention and love as well as sexual union whenever he wishes. This gives him a kind of pride and satisfaction at being married, and he feels grateful toward society for allowing him to enjoy it without much effort on his part. It's nice to have a real woman around who offers herself mentally and sexually to him alone, rather than having to satisfy himself vicariously through others' experiences or reading, movies, or perhaps a few sporadic, sneaking experiences with unrespectable women. If he is inexperienced, as is usually the case, his nervousness adds to the intrigue even more.

The "flower bed" night for the wife is very important because this is the beginning of her married state. The particular night, however, does not loom as large as it does in the mind of her husband. She pushes away the thought of sex a bit nervously, even though she has been hearing lots of stories about the pains and pleasures of the first experience. She tries to exaggerate the pleasure and she waits to give herself to her god and lover. The disappointment that may be a result of both inexperience and too many romantic expectations does not shatter her because she hopes for the future. She is also too shy to enjoy the sexual part of it, no matter how much she fantasized before. For example:

Case no. 22: Yes, I remember my "flower bed" night very well. This is a very significant night for all girls, as you know. Although I was rather tired from the trip the same morning from my hometown, and sad from the separation from my family, I looked forward to the evening with great expectation and nervousness mixed with pleasure. I tried to visualize the beautiful nuptial bed decorated with all the flowers of the season waiting for us, my husband and me. Something, I cannot remember exactly what, delayed my father's friend in the same town, to bring the flowers, which were really supposed to be sent by my family. So when the flowers arrived, it was already quite late. One of my husband's sisters decorated the bed with lots of lotus, roses, and tuberoses, and by the time we went through a couple of short ceremonies and finally were ready to go to our bedroom, a woman, someone from the guests, pushed me inside the room and locked the door from outside. My husband, whom I hardly knew still, was alone with me in the room. He bolted the door from inside and muttered something about being tired and began to take off the flower garland and his scarf. He also gathered the huge bedspread full of fresh and fragrant flowers—hundreds of them—and made a clumsy bundle before he dropped it on the floor. I was sad and did not know why, disappointed to see the flowers crushed. They were supposed to be crushed by our bodies, I supposed. My husband told me that he was too tired and sleepy and asked me to rest. He turned around and fell asleep. For a long time I sat on the edge of the big bed in my jewelry, heavy silk sari, and the flower decoration on my head. I was very tired but did not go to sleep. Looking at my husband's tired figure, I felt sorry but I was also disappointed, as if I expected that night to be something else. A couple of nights later, I remember, after my husband showed more attention and willingness to get closer to me, I even forgot about the "flower bed" evening. But, later, years later, when I spent several nights awake in bed wondering about my life, my husband, and the unknown unhappiness

I experienced, I again thought of that night. Something told me that the whole thing began with that night. I regretted that it was not a memorable night for me as it is for most women, I assume.

Apart from the sexual expectations, the husband feels happy to have acquired a wife because of what he has been taught. The wedding indicates to him the beginning of a status that he likes. Sooner or later this woman will bear him a child, and he will become a father, another fulfillment of his social role. He also feels quite powerful because he owns this woman who left her whole family to be his wife and part of his family. She becomes a symbol of the future prosperity and happiness of himself and his family. It is as if he has performed his duty toward his family in bringing her to them, despite the fact that he had little to do with acquiring her. If she happens to be beautiful and comes from a good family, his friends and relatives talk about it, which makes him proud too. They always mention her as his wife, as if he deserves some credit for her beauty and youth and presentable background. It is important that the others, particularly his family, like her. If she pleases everybody, he will have peace and happiness. He needs to respect her as a person because soon she will be a mother, a role more respectable than enjoyable. Also, it is easier for him to relate to her that way. In fact, he feels rather strange and uncertain about their relationship till she becomes pregnant. During his upbringing he never learned how to feel romantic toward his future wife. He has already built up a close friendship with some hint of romanticism with his distant cousins and sisters-in-law, or perhaps some friends' wives. For the time being, he feels close to her and looks forward to meeting her at night in bed. He even enjoys small things such as *pān* (betel-leaf) made by her or a cup of tea that she brings to his bed in the morning. He enjoys her shyness and the sparkle in her eyes as he makes small advances. It is a great feeling that there is a young woman in the house who is ready to give her whole life for him. In short, the marriage for him does not come with all the rainbow colors of fantasy and romance that it does for his wife. Moreover, his needs for affection, emotion, and love may continue to be satisfied by his other female relatives, his mother and sisters. From his wife he does not particularly expect these. He rather likes, as the custom goes, the idea of being a distant figure of worship for her.

The fact that a married woman begins to feel frustrated very soon in her marriage has a lot to do with the husband's qualitatively different expectations concerning their relationship. Let me touch briefly on the early life of a Bengali man. For a growing male child in an upper-class Bengali family all women he comes in contact with are believed to fall in the respectable category of "mothers" (*māyer jāti*). Ideally, within the realm of his extended family world, he is not expected to encounter any women (unchaste women, prostitutes) who can be enjoyed for physical pleasure alone. The sexual knowledge that a young boy in such families begins to receive from his male friends, cousins, and perhaps manservants, along with the illustrated pornography that his friends provide him with, teaches him that sexual desire, although dirty and undesirable, promises something pleasurable when experienced. The women he can experience such pleasure with are, of course, not the women he learns to respect, but the ones who are outside that category. In a society where a strong sexual taboo operates so that the information on sex does not come either through institutionalized means or through adult relatives as a part of natural learning, the message a growing Bengali youth receives from indirect sources becomes distorted. He does not learn to consider sexual pleasure as being natural and to be associated with women he considers respectable.

Second, he never learns that his future wife is the person who will fulfill all his romantic needs. The fact that marriage for him does not involve separation from his family is the third point that makes it unnecessary for him to expect love from his spouse. His wife loses her father's love, which has been so important to her. The first person she depends upon for compensation is the husband. For him, who has the assurance of the lifelong reservoir of love from his mother, sisters, and sisters-in-law, the need for romantic love is not as crucial as his wife's.

Husband-Wife Interaction

As for her relationship with her husband for the first year of her marriage, apart from sleeping together, the new bride may have very little contact with him during the daytime. Usually she gets up in the morning and leaves the bedroom before he wakes up. There is tacit disapproval in the eyes of the family if the new bride does not finish her early morning bath and toilet before her husband and older relatives do. She is often expected to make tea or at least to serve it to the others in bed. If her mother-in-law is an early riser (and most of them are), she may be expected to join her in preparing her daily worship or to give a hand in the kitchen in the preparation of breakfast by the servants. She may sneak out for a few minutes to wake her husband with a cup of tea, while she also makes his bath ready. Her morning duties include helping with the preparation and serving of breakfast and helping the mother-in-law or the older sisters-in-law in the preparation of the noon meal, the major meal in a Bengali home. She may chop vegetables or supervise the maids as they grind the spices. She may also have to supervise the breakfast of the servants and the children and give a hand in bathing and preparing the younger children for school.

When her husband comes to the kitchen all ready to go to work, it is usually his mother (if he happens to be a favorite son) who looks after his needs. His mother may just sit near the dining area with a small hand-fan to drive away flies or to cool off the steaming food while chatting with her sons who are eating and getting ready for work. The new bride may be summoned to serve the dishes while the mother-in-law keeps a keen eye on her ways. She may give her occasional instructions, saying, "Give your older brother-in-law another fish head, he loves them." Or, "Go get some more hot rice, don't you see that your husband's dish is empty?" Through all this, the bride receives information as to who likes what to eat and to whom she has to be most attentive when serving food because he is the favorite son of the mother. She learns this easily enough from the amount of pressure the mother puts on the son to eat more, because in Bengal, and perhaps all over India, feeding is the principal technique of women, no matter what age they may be, to show affection and love to their men. Food is also used as the means to show the withdrawal of love. It is a very common technique for the husband to say he has no appetite if he wishes to punish his wife or his mother. Children are rewarded and punished with food or the withholding of it.

The bride begins to see a pattern in the household through such domestic services, and this helps her make small adjustments to the members of the family. The adjustment is easy if she is intelligent enough to grasp the lines of cleavage between allies and enemies, and to act tactfully. She must know who the important persons are and please those persons while not antagonizing the others. This requires keen observation and tact. Once she is able to do this she has her reward. She will be liked by the important factions and left alone by the less important ones. She also receives subtle reinforcements in the form of praise if she behaves like a good daughter-in-law.

After the men finish eating their noon meal, her next duty may be to make or serve the *pān* (betel-leaf and nut, which is chewed in such households after every meal), and at this time she may have another chance to see her husband alone for a few seconds when she brings him the *pān*. They may have a very brief exchange of smiles, a look, and a split-second's touch when she hands the *pān* to him. He may even allow her to put it directly into his mouth while he is tying his shoelaces or combing his hair before hurrying out to work. She enjoys such momentary touches and communication. But this may not be possible in some families where the *pān* may be served by the mother herself or one of the sisters-in-law who has been doing it for a long time.

After the men and the younger people depart for work and school or college, the daughter-in-law may have to prepare her father-in-law's bath or take him a late morning cup of tea. She may exchange a few words with him or help him with writing a letter or reading the headlines of the newspaper. She may also give him a head massage with oil before his bath. She may also be expected to serve his meal and wait on him. After the old man is fed and the babies are put to noon nap, the women begin to eat their lunch. They all sit together and enjoy their lunch slowly while chatting about the neighbors and other small matters. They may plan the snacks for tea in the afternoon or plan on going out for a matinee. The women have leisure after lunch for three or four hours. The new daughter-in-law may take a nap or chat with her younger sisters-in-law or some young wives from the neighborhood. She may also be summoned by her mother-in-law to read aloud until she falls asleep.

The new daughter-in-law's next contact with her husband is during the afternoon tea when he comes back from work, and again this is in the presence of others in the family. She may accompany him to a few engagements to which they are invited by friends and relatives soon after the wedding. This is the chance for her to spend an evening outside the family. They may be alone in a car or a taxi or a bus. They may even go to an evening movie or two, but it is customary to take a sister-in-law with them; otherwise, it might appear a shameless flaunting of social custom. Only if they are invited out by the husband's office colleagues with whom the family is not acquainted may he take her alone. Other than that, she seldom spends the evenings alone with her husband. He may continue to visit his male friends or their families for chitchat[5] and come home around dinner time in the late evening. At night in the bedroom they are alone at last. Sometimes she may come late after taking care of her evening duties, being with the older people in the kitchen, supervising the children's dinner, and so on. It is considered bad manners for her to retire before at least the older relatives have gone to bed. She has to pretend sometimes that she is in no hurry when she is trying to put an insomniac father-in-law to sleep by massaging his head or reading him some monotonous book. She may tiptoe back to the bedroom only when the old man begins to snore. Her allies in this matter, her younger sisters-in-law who have also been sufferers, help her in this and try to manipulate the situation so that she is released earlier. (But this help may be available only for the first few months of marriage.) Her husband, meanwhile, waits in bed, smokes, and perhaps falls asleep while cursing the complications of the joint-family. If this becomes routine, he may not bother to wait and may find something else to do—going out after dinner for another chat with his friends or involving himself in some kind of hobby such as acting or music or evening sports at the neighborhood club. At any rate, by the time his wife manages to come to the bedroom without raising too many eyebrows, she may find him half-asleep. They have very little to talk about anyway; all she can tell him at this stage of their marriage will be her disappointments with him and perhaps with the *sasur-bāri*. And she knows she should not talk this way so early in her marriage. He on his part has little to talk about, except his office or a street scene that he may have witnessed while coming home. He is interested in having her sexually and does not feel like wasting time with trivial chat.

He even enjoys the resentment (a pose, he is sure) she displays every night when he approaches her. They never discuss the sexual act with each other, because no one is supposed to talk about such things, even husband and wife. If she is bold and aggressive enough to take the initiative and talk about the only act they share, she may create a very unfavorable impression. She is expected to be modest above all other considerations. Therefore, the married couple engages in sexual intercourse in a matter-of-fact way without much attempt to make it seem an act of pleasure, even though they may very well enjoy it. Within a few days she notices a difference between her expectations about the exalting experience she read about and her real experience. Her flower-bed evening was only a glimmering of some promise that was never realized. Often she wonders if her newly married aunts and brothers' wives in her father's home had the same experience or is she the only one? She cannot tell from looking at them what exactly went on except for a few very subtle suggestions that they were happy and as if in love. Consider the following case, for example.

Case no. 23: During the first couple of months of my marriage, I discovered that sleeping with my husband was something I should not ask for. I fell in love with him so intensely from the very night of our wedding that my whole day was spent dreaming about meeting him at night. If ever he came home early or ran into me alone on the veranda, I felt as though I were going through an electric shock. My heart began to beat fast. I looked for every opportunity to be with him, near him. If he ever said a word to me alone, I was so elated. I always expected him to talk to me when I came to bed at night. I hoped he would take a personal interest in me, that he would ask how my day went, whether I needed anything. I also missed my father who dis- cussed his office problems with me. I wondered why my husband had nothing to talk about. I often asked him questions about his work, his colleagues, his friends. I tried to imagine his life outside home. I began to feel I was not at all as important to him as I was to my father or even to my older brothers. He did not need me as they did. I also felt he did not know me and did not care. He wanted sex often but never when I felt like it. I never could be so shameless as to tell him that, but it became a routine thing. When we had sex I closed my eyes and tried to feel very happy and afterward tried to think how all those women in the books felt. Was it really different with Rādhā or Juliet? If so, what was missing in my case? Often I kept thinking this for hours while my husband slept and snored. Yet during the day my giggling sister-in-law would ask me very straight questions about our sex life, how exactly he approached me, and so on. I felt ashamed to tell her the truth and avoided the answer by feigning shyness. Let them imagine what they wanted. I wondered if they did not have the same experience. I never found out.

The minimal contact with her husband during the day increases the intensity of her expectations for closer contact during the night. Unfortunately, it is never realized. The romantic expectations she had built up about the marriage before she was married and reinforced by occasional promises soon after marriage all seem unreal and remote by the time she has been married for six or seven months. Even the act of sexual inter-course becomes either a regular routine or infrequent. This period of dwindling hopes, followed by frustrations, followed by further expectations, goes on for a longer time if the contact between the husband and the wife is less than usual due to occasional separation. She may go away for short visits to her father or to attend family weddings or funerals. Or he may go away on business trips. It is not rare in this part of Bengali society for the husband to go abroad to study for a couple of years soon after the wedding. Sometimes a wedding with a handsome cash dowry is planned to help finance his trip to a foreign university. In such cases, he may make his wife pregnant before leaving (so that she keeps busy while he is away) or she may simply wait at home for two or three years weaving her lingering dreams and expectations until he comes back. In such cases her expectations are postponed for two or three years. She may be allowed to spend part of her lonely time at her father's home while the husband is away gathering academic and perhaps extra-academic experience in a relatively free society.[6] If she happens to be pregnant before he leaves, she is more fortunate, because most of her time will be taken up by her child. This period of waiting may also be very crucial for her in building up platonic romantic relationships with the younger male members of the household, namely her husband's younger brothers. Cases of a husband leaving for education abroad are not altogether frequent and her relationship with her brothers-in-law may be encouraged irrespective of his presence. They are always the younger brothers because she must practice a subtle rule of avoidance of her older male relatives by marriage, including her older brothers-in-law.

Other Male Relatives by Marriage

Ideally, a woman is supposed to observe the custom of avoidance with her older male relatives. In practice, she treats them with respect and some distance, not total avoidance. She may not address them directly if she can avoid doing so. But she may spend some time every day listening to her father-in-law or talking to one of her older brothers-in-law. The distance may be said to increase with the decreasing age of those who are older than her husband. This rule reverses totally for those younger than her husband. With her father-in-law she spends more time chatting, reading to him, or massaging his feet or head. With her older brothers-in-law, this would be considered totally indiscreet. She always covers her head with the end of her sari to symbolize respect whenever she is in the presence of her older male relatives. The attitude of the older brothers-in-law may be summarized as follows. They tried to find a good girl for their brother (who needed to be tied down because otherwise he would get out of hand), and they believe they did their duty in finding a girl from a good family. The rest depends on the luck of the brother and the family, and only the future will tell. The older males may be quite aware of the physical attractiveness of this young woman in the household, but they are not supposed to have such thoughts about a younger brother's wife. They are thankful for the custom of avoidance and distance; this helps. Besides, a young wife in the household is not of great concern to them as long as she can keep their mother and their wives reasonably happy and satisfy their brother. They may give the girl serious thought only if the mother, or one of the older wives, begins to complain about her conduct.

The Mother-in-law

"Mother-in-law" in such a household does not refer to the mother of the husband alone; it is a category that may include one or several classificatory mothers-in-law such as a widowed sister of the father-in-law or a wife of the father-in-law's brother. One of these women may replace the true mother-in-law if she dies; they are, in any case, much in evidence. In other words, a newly married woman finds herself in contact with more than one mother-in-law. Her expected behavior to all of them appears to be the same. There is no avoidance of these women. Ideally, in this section of Bengali society, the mother-in-law is supposed to treat her daughter-in-law like her own daughter. However, in reality, the quality of behavior is determined by several factors, the personalities of the two being the most important. The mother-in-law may take a great fancy to the new daughter-in-law if she happens to be a nice girl, especially if she comes from a rich and well-known family and, more important, if she has brought a valuable dowry with her. If she is married to the favorite son, the relationship may be slightly tense as well as close. She also may be liked by her husband's mother because she is pretty and modest and obedient. [7] From the daughter-in-law's point of view, the old lady does not replace her own mother, as the ideal says she should, but she accepts her as her husband's mother and a close relation to her develops. If they are friends, it will be considered fortunate; if they cannot get along, it is unfortunate and the sanction will always be against the daughter-in-law. So it is the daughter-in-law's responsibility to make an effort to get along with her husband's mother. In return, she often receives affection and a strong ally in the joint household.

The tension in the relationship between the mother and the wife of a single son, however, can reach a point where the wife's relationship with her husband is affected. If the mother is very close to her son and feels possessive about him, the creeping disappointment of the wife's expectations about her marriage can be aggravated to a great extent. She observes that his mother has more hold over the son, and that her love for him is well acknowledged and demonstratively returned. She has more access to her son's affection and love than his wife does. A wife faced with this condition over and above her already mounting disappointment finds this difficult to bear. She feels competitive toward his mother. It is as if the wife would have been better off as a mother to her husband than as a wife.

Case no. 24: When I was first married I craved to do more things for my husband. But I knew that in a big household like ours he had many relatives to look after him and his needs. The things I used to do for my father, like deciding which shirt he should wear, folding and ironing his handkerchiefs, keeping his cigarettes and matches in place, opening his letters and sometimes replying to them, and thousands of other things—all I missed not doing. My father-in-law did not need me for this. He had a college-going granddaughter who looked after his small needs and, besides, he stayed home most of the time doing nothing but dozing over some book. My husband had his mother, his sisters, and his sisters-in-law to take care of all his needs. I felt almost completely left out. I often watched him go to his *sej boudi's* [third sister-in-law] room and let her fix his button or let her help him with his cuff links. He would ask me only if there was something to be done while we both happened to be in the bedroom together. I think he was shy to approach me in the presence of the others. I also felt rather jealous when he took his sisters to the movies or spent hours chatting with his *sej boudi*, joking and teasing her.

Case no. 25: My husband was hardly home. Sometimes he would come back from his office very late in the evening. Everybody in the house seemed to have accepted this habit. In fact, his sisters teased him a lot after our marriage because he came home early for a few days. They joked about it as if he was changing his lifelong habits because of his new wife. To this my husband smiled with embarrassment, and soon went back to the old habit as if to please everybody. He did not come back in the afternoon to have tea at all. He would come home at nine or ten in the evening. My mother-in-law would stay up with his dinner, which she kept warm in a kerosene stove. I also waited with her even though I felt I was not needed. From the conversation the son and the mother had over his dinner, I could gather that he went to visit a particular cousin and his wife almost every evening. He also went to certain office-clubs to play cards. I felt very envious of those unknown people he spent so much time with.

Some evenings, if the mother-in-law could not stay up so late, I would stay alone and I liked such occasions when I was alone to wait upon him. This gave me so much satisfaction that even if he told me that he was late because he went to see a movie with his cousin's wife, I tried not to feel bad. But occasions like this happened rarely, because my mother-in-law felt hesitant to leave the whole responsibility to me. Sometimes, after dinner, my husband would go to his mother's room and spend a couple of hours there just lying next to her putting his arms around her and chatting. Some nights he even fell asleep there and would come to bed very late almost half-asleep. I could only weep and blame my fate to be married to a son so close to his mother. Later, when I thought about this, I was surprised at myself that while in my father's home I never noticed such closeness between my brothers and my mother. Perhaps my brothers' wives felt the same way as I did now.

Thus the new wife discovers that the relationship that lasts longer than any other is between the mother and the son. She almost consciously wishes to become a mother.

The Older Sisters-in-law

With her older sisters-in-law, who have already reached positions of higher authority because of their age and seniority, she has a somewhat distant relationship. Ideally, the older sisters-in-law are like her own sisters. In practice, she feels tinges of jealousy toward some of them, particularly if one of them happens to be close to her husband or close to the mother-in-law. There is also a subtle competition involved among these women because of their different backgrounds and looks, which may have determined their positions in this family to begin with. The mother-in-law may favor a particular daughter-in-law because of her attractive background and looks. While the older daughters-in-law are envious of the new one because of her youth and position with the mother-in-law, the new one is envious of the older ones because of their established positions in the household and their hold over some of the male members, including perhaps her husband.

The Younger Sisters-in-law

Her relationship with her younger sisters-in-law (husband's brothers' wives who are close to her age, and the husband's unmarried sisters) is usually one of friendship and cordiality. But there may be some tension involved because of her relationship with the unmarried sisters of the husband, particularly if he is close to them. This jealousy, which may be considerable, may not find expressions in overt behavior. The *boudi* (sister-in-law) tolerates it to a great extent, because she knows that in a Bengali home brothers and sisters are supposed to be extremely close. She herself has been and still is very close to her own brothers. But like most situations of emotional stress, understanding does not necessarily reduce the pain.

Case no. 26: My husband has always been close to his only sister. When I was married, I could sense that my *nanad* [husband's sister] did not like me, even though she was quite nice in her behavior. I could see that she became tense if my husband took an interest in me or brought a gift for me. It never happened that he would bring something for me without bringing something for her also. When he brought two saris for the *Pujā*, I always let my *nanad* choose first. . . . At night, she would often come and chat in our room and linger for a while, lying on our bed close to her brother, sometimes tickling him or teasing him by pulling an imaginary gray hair. All this was quite innocent, I realized; but somehow it bothered me. I could not help feeling that she lingered in our room so late because she disliked the idea of my sharing the night with her brother. Something seemed not quite right in her intrusions. I could not recall doing this to my brother when he was first married, even though we were very close. . . . Later, I heard from a neighbor that my *nanad* was disappointed when the marriage proposal between her brother and me was arranged. She wanted one of her close friends to become her *boudi*. She, I think, resented that her brother did not have all the time for her anymore. Well, I consoled myself by thinking that she would be married sooner or later.

Thus the *boudi* tolerates the situation as mentioned above, because (1) the *nanad* leaves the household sooner or later and (2) she knows that as an outsider she has no right to interfere with the brother-sister relationship, which is a lifelong bond of dependence and friendship. Her jealousy and resentment about one of the sisters-in-law, on the other hand, may be deeper and less tolerable. But again, she cannot do anything about it, except by avenging the situation by bringing a brother-in-law close to herself. (This may be done quite unconsciously, however.) But more on that later.

The wives of her husband's brothers who are close to her age are often in the same state she is. They may be suffering from the same sexual and emotional frustrations and disillusionment about marriage. Of course, the intensity of such frustration will vary according to the personalities of the women. The women usually get together after the midday meal and have long chats. The topics of discussion range from complaints against the mother-in-law to their individual husbands in the bedrooms. A great amount of giggling and fun goes on when they tease one another to find out the real stories of their bedrooms. These sessions are also attended by other young wives of the neighborhood. The purpose seems to be an unconscious desire to share one another's experiences even though not all of them are aware of it or are very open about it. Some do not have the ability to analyze their feelings and may even be quite happy in their own way. Such wives may be called "*swāmi shohāgini*," a term meaning "the husband's favorite." They talk a lot, and this gossip, which washes the dirty linen of others, gives satisfaction. The new wife may also spend drowsy noons reading novels and magazines. She finds reading love stories particularly stimulating and pleasing. Women exchange such books among themselves. She also listens to the noon radio program designed for housewives. The program usually includes a very sentimental short story in which a woman is rejected in love, sacrifices her life for it, and so on. There are also cooking recipes or sewing patterns and a couple of sentimental love songs. In short, these noon sessions of a young wife perhaps compensate for her nighttime frustrations. These sessions tell her that she is not alone in her frustrated life and, of course, offer her the vicarious pleasure of listening to others' loves and lives. She also finds a number of friends among the women in whom she may confide her secrets. One of her *nanads* (husband's cousins) may be a very close friend who follows her around. The *nanad* likes the idea of being around a newly married woman who has supposedly tasted the bliss and pleasure of marriage. She is also intrigued by her jewelry and saris, which she may borrow to wear when she goes out with her girl friends to weddings or movies. Such a friendship between a *boudi* and a *nanad* happens provided that she is not the only sister (and therefore a very close one) to her brother and that both women have friendly personalities and a need for each other.

The Brother-in-law

The most significant relative for the newly married woman in her *sasur-bāri* is her husband's younger brother (*debar*). The *debar-boudi* relationship is of close friendship and tenderness. If she happens to have a *debar* close to her age, they may easily become close friends. If he is a lot younger she is still close to him, but treats him more like a younger brother. Her daily interaction with her *debar*, in terms of fulfilling certain duties, is minimal, because he holds a position in the family that is somewhat limited and a married woman has no prescribed obligation to look after his needs as she must do with other relatives. As a result, she gets to know him slowly and perhaps last in the course of her first couple of weeks' stay in her *sasur-bāri*. Also, the *debar* is shy about approaching her. He knows that ideally he should treat his *boudi* as a mother and an older sister. He should respect her and expect affection in return. But her age, her entry into the family as an outsider, and also her apparent loneliness all attract him toward her in a way that cannot be clearly defined. In order to understand the nature of this attraction, one also has to see his position and condition in the family. He is not a son who has an established job and of an age to be considered as one of the decision-making males; but he is not the young son, either, who needs his mother's constant attention. He may be a student or may have a job, but he is not an active and effective member of the family because he is not yet married and responsible. Except for a few younger sisters, he has had little contact with girls of his age. His curiosity about women is usually satisfied indirectly by the information his peers provide him or through books and movies. He is not told enough to grasp the real nature of heterosexual relationship, but at the same time he is intrigued by it. At this stage he "finds" his *boudi* who is young, most probably attractive (in such families, marriages are rarely contracted if the bride is not good-looking), [8] and warm toward him (because she misses her own cousins and brothers). It is not difficult for him to become her admirer very soon. Despite the lack of frequent contact and interaction between the two, this often happens quickly, due to the absence of familial restriction against such closeness. Rather, it is often encouraged: nobody says anything against a *debar* who worships his *boudi* or a *boudi* who showers her affection on her *debar*. The terms "worship" and "affection" are intentional, because that is the way it is expressed by the people in the family and by the participants themselves. Ideally, a *debar-boudi* relationship should be one of worship and affection. However, their individual positions in this joint-family, where both are emotionally lonely, their ages and sexes, plus their ideas about romantic love, all work together to bring them emotionally close to each other. Let's take the *boudi's* situation first.

From her interactions with her various relatives, including her husband, it is clear that the newly married woman is deprived of the kind of love she expected to get from her husband and from the marriage as a whole. For the most important of her affective relationships in her natal home, namely her father's love, neither her husband nor her father-in-law appear to offer the replacement. As for her romantic expectations, the husband again does not offer satisfaction to any effective extent. She also misses her brothers and the cousins who gave her companionship during the last two or three years of adolescence in her father's home. Her expectations of love, based on the combination of a male figure of father, husband-lover, and brother that she so eagerly hoped to receive from her marriage are not realized, although she may occasionally receive a sampling of all these from her male relatives. Her husband, for example, may offer her the distant authority that her father partly represented, and the father-in-law may offer part of the need of dependence on her that her father had, but neither forms a total satisfaction. Her husband offers the sexual part of love without the associated romantic exaltation that she dreamed of experiencing, and the husband definitely is not around to give her the flirtatious and, at the same time, affectionate friendship her brothers and cousins offered her. It appears almost a logical outcome that she become emotionally close to her *debar* who offers her the possibilities of at least the second two relationships. The *debar* is around to receive her love and affection that she has hopelessly prepared to offer her husband.

From the *debar's* point of view, he has found the perfect woman to whom he can look up with admiration and can be sure of the security of emotion and affection that he does not at the moment receive from his mother or older sisters. His mother is too busy with the household and the older brothers, the sisters are too busy with their households and not even around to show affection. Besides, this woman, unrelated by blood, with her youth and attractiveness, satisfies his desire to become close to a woman, a natural desire for his age that is not satisfied by society as a whole. If he had opportunities to know women outside his family, perhaps his need to know her and to reciprocate her affection and love would not be so strong. His somewhat undefined and unnoticed presence in the family makes him look to at least one person for a special existence.

Thus a bond develops rather fast, particularly if the *boudi* is attractive and warm. Gradually, they find occasions and excuses to be together more often. The *debar* talks to her about his friends, his dreams about his future, and his loneliness. His *boudi* is always very patient with him; she gives him a hearing and occasional indulgence. He, in turn, carries out her small requests such as getting her the right colored wool for her knitting or getting a few novels from the neighborhood public library. He does this with great pleasure. He wishes she would give him more opportunities to prove his worth. It makes him feel important that she makes requests of him, rather than someone else. From her side she is grateful that there is someone in the whole household who has time to look after her needs and wishes. She tells him about her childhood, her brothers and sisters, and her life in her father's home. Thus develops a relationship in which it is clear to both partners that the love they share is not quite the love a sister has for a brother or vice versa. Yet, it is also not something a husband and a wife are supposed to share. Since the closeness between the two is totally acceptable by the family and society, the relationship continues. The women in the family, who are the only ones to watch them becoming such close friends, do not object because this is in the nature of things. They all in their turn have had *debars* (at least classificatory ones), and they know from experience that there is nothing wrong in it, unless a clear-cut love affair develops. And this happens rarely, because neither the *boudi* nor the *debar* is interested in an overt love affair. The relationship satisfies certain needs for both people, and the undefined nature of it is perhaps essential for it to continue. When the *debar* gets married the relationship may suffer from the fact that they cannot spend so much time together, but given the custom of distance between the husband and wife the *boudi* in fact does not lose the *debar's* company to any large extent. She accepts the new wife without much resentment because this is the custom and, second, she is sure of her bond with her *debar* even though there is a newcomer in between. She knows that the years she and her *debar* shared cannot be wiped out so easily, and the needs she fulfilled for him cannot be fulfilled by his wife. So it is the wife, rather than the *boudi*, who feels left out, till she finds a *debar* of her own, at least for a number of years to come.

The reasons that this relationship rarely becomes sexual may be manifold. Sex, or the desire to be sexually involved, may often be repressed because of the general pattern of sexual behavior in Bengal and India in general. Second, the wife is sexually active with her husband, even though sexual activity may not be as total and satisfying as it might have been. From the *debar's* point of view, the same repression operates and in the image of a *boudi* that he has been taught to internalize, sexual attraction is anything but conscious. As a growing man he knows that sex is used with one's married wife to have children, and though sex can be enjoyed with a prostitute or a woman of lower class or caste, it is not a nice thing, anyway. His love and adoration for his *boudi*, who is a combination of his mother, elder sister, and a romantic companion and friend, cannot and should not induce the thought of having sexual contact with her. He represses the thought completely unless the circumstances produce a very special situation.

There are such exceptional cases. In the case of a young widowed *boudi* without children, the relationship may turn into a sexual one. In such cases, members of the household try to suppress the information so that the neighbors will not find out. What is important is not the act as much as the disapproval of society, which stigmatizes the honor of the family. A newly married wife, left behind by a husband who plans on higher education abroad immediately after the wedding, may also become her *debar's* mistress. But this may not happen unless conditions in the household create stimulating factors for such an affair. For example, if the elders (especially the women) are indifferent and callous enough to leave the couple completely alone, and the members of the family are so few that both the *debar* and the *boudi* have no other person to be close to, and if both of them are more independent than usual in their attitudes concerning sex relationships, an overt sexual affair may develop. Consider the following case, for instance.

Case no. 27: When I was married I had to leave M.P. [Madhya Pradesh] where my father worked as a doctor and come all the way to north Bengal with my husband who was a shareholder in a tea plantation. I was sad to find that I would have to live there in the midst of a tea garden with no family around. I came from a family of seven brothers and sisters and I felt completely lost in that quiet land where all you could see were tea bushes. My husband had a beautiful bungalow and half-a-dozen servants to keep me comfortable. The nearest neighbor was a mile away, the only other family, the manager who was from south India and his wife, did not speak Bengali or English. The doctor of the plantation was Bengali, but they lived four miles away. My mother-in-law lived with us, but she was very old and quiet. Most of the time she was busy worshiping her god in the corner of her bedroom or she would read *The Rāmāyana* or write letters to her relatives in Calcutta. We never became close to each other, even though I knew that she liked me quite a bit. She was a kind of person who liked everybody but was not involved particularly, you know what I mean? She was surely very different from both my own mother and my grandmother. She became a widow early in life and learned to be alone and quiet.

So you see, my image of a *sasur-bāri* was very different from what I found. I missed my large family where we had lots of fun together. My husband, who was busy with his work in the factory eight to nine hours every day, was also a very quiet man. He was very kind and nice and I could tell that he was worried about me because I was lonely in that big bungalow. He bought me lots of records and books to keep me company; he even mentioned many times that he was not a talker and if I felt too bored I could go to Calcutta for a while. But I did not like the idea to leave him alone. I admired his devotion to his work and I also respected him as a person who was so kind-hearted. But I was bored all the same. My husband had several younger brothers and sisters who were going to schools and colleges in Calcutta and since the tea garden had no good school I could not even suggest that we have one of his brothers or sisters with us to keep me company.

After about four months, when I was bored to tears and could not amuse myself with novels or records or anything, one day my husband came back from his work and told my mother-in-law happily that his brother was about to return from England. I knew that his next brother had been studying in England for several years. My husband also told us that Rabi [his brother] decided to come to the tea garden first to see the new *boudi* and spend a few weeks with us before going to Calcutta to visit the larger family. There was a possibility that he might get a job offer at the next plantation where they needed an engineer. This news delighted me just because there would be a new face in the house. I was also curious to meet this *debar* of mine about whom I heard so much. It pleased me to know that he was so eager to meet me. The news also pleased my husband and mother-in-law very much. Rabi was a very close brother of my husband's. It was my husband who paid for his education in England. We all looked forward to his arrival. . . . When Rabi came I was struck by the dissimilarity between the two brothers. Unlike my husband, who was quiet, reserved, and calm, Rabi was talkative, lively, and restless. He talked incessantly, laughing, joking, and making others laugh at the same time. When we met he objected to touching my feet as the sign of respect in traditional fashion because he claimed that he was a year older, even though I was older by relationship. He put his arms around me instead, to my great surprise, I guess in European style. His mother and brother both smiled at his childlike behavior. The mother mentioned that even four years abroad could not change her son's childlike nature and she left to supervise the cooking to make the dishes Rabi liked. For several days we had continuous festival; while my

mother-in-law was busy helping the cook prepare all the dishes
Rabi liked, I was busy attending to his comfort and listening to
his talk about his life in England. He followed me everywhere to
talk; sometimes stretching on my bed, sometimes reclining on the
couch, sometimes walking beside me while I cut flowers from the
garden. The whole atmosphere of the household changed. He
kept everybody busy and happy. He joked with the cooks, teased
the young maid, and made fun of his mother about her little deity
in the corner of her bedroom.

I began to feel as if I lived for the first time. I told my husband
how happy I was that Rabi had come to visit us. My husband
looked very pleased and told me that he would see to it that he
got the job in the factory of the next garden. . . . Thus it all began.
We all were suddenly happy together. A couple of weeks after
Rabi's arrival my older brother-in-law became very ill and we got
a telegram from Calcutta. My husband decided to take the
mother and fly immediately. Rabi just began his new job, so he
could not go and naturally I was to stay to look after him. They
were away for three weeks and during this time we became
lovers. It all happened as if automatically. I found to my great
pleasure that making love could be utter happiness, which I
never experienced before. I discovered for the first time that I did
not love my husband but his brother. Rabi kindled something in
me that did not exist between my husband and me. Those three
weeks were all joy and happiness. I became his slave; he treated
me as a friend, as an equal, and resented being treated as
someone I looked up to. But I could not think of him as anything
but my real husband. This thought was a pleasure as well as a
pain. I could not help feeling very guilty. Rabi also knew the art
of flattering. He often compared me with the foreign girls he
knew and told me how wonderful I was. . . . Then one day came
the telegram from Calcutta that my brother-in-law had died and
Rabi and I must leave immediately for the funeral. I felt very sad
and extremely guilty as if my action had something to do with his
death. I began to suffer from a bad conscience and I told Rabi
that we must stop otherwise the whole family was going to be
ruined. I never believed in fate so much as I did then. But it was
impossible to get away from his attraction. I thought of suggesting
a marriage for him; but the death in the family would make it
impossible at least for a year. While in Calcutta, the grief in the
family distracted me and I could forget the whole thing for the
time being. I felt very close and sympathetic toward my widowed
sister-in-law. After the *shrāddha* [the ceremony after ten days]

we came back to the plantation again. My mother-in-law decided to stay with her widowed daughter-in-law and the children in Calcutta. I was quite frightened because there would not be any restriction then; I was also happy at the same time. I was also frightened because Rabi did not seem to worry over the matter the way I did. He had no problem loving his brother as before. He never admitted any sense of guilt about this. This made me feel rather alone in the whole business of suffering. Often I wanted to confess to my husband, but I could not bring myself to do so. After about a month he began to suspect, but as his nature was, he did not say anything. He just became cold to me. He began to come home even later than usual and went to bed sooner. We hardly exchanged a word. His behavior to his brother did not change. He just looked more tired and quieter.

The atmosphere in the house changed considerably from a gay, happy one to a cold, stifling one. Even Rabi did not seem as lively as before. He looked as if he began to suffer also, even though he never admitted it. I began to avoid him and my husband both and tried to pray to the deity my mother-in-law left behind in her room. How I cried to God and asked for forgiveness and wished I could go back to those days when I was bored and lonely but not so unhappy. But it was too late.

To end the story the woman had a child about five years after her marriage. Malicious relatives gossiped that the child looked more like the uncle than the father. The *debar* married and moved to Calcutta with a new job. The woman continued a poor attempt at playing the role of a good wife. Perhaps she became a good mother, her only escape under the circumstances. She did not tell me about this clearly. But the birth of the child is important. If it was by the *debar* and the husband knew about it, it is interesting that he decided to accept it, perhaps for the sake of the good name of the family. If the child was the husband's, it is also interesting that the husband did not mind having the child with an unfaithful wife. Was it because he did not want any talk or was it because he hoped a child would cure her problem? It is also interesting that the relationship between the two brothers never became strained. Unfortunately, I do not have the husband's side of the story. It would have been interesting to know if his indifference toward any romantic relationship with his wife was so deep-seated as to allow him to ignore her extramarital affair, or was it his brotherly love and obligation that made him tolerate the betrayal? Knowing Bengali society, my guess would be that both operated and perhaps in this case the second was more important than the first.

This example is the only one in my data where a clear-cut sexual affair was admitted and, as can be seen, is quite a unique one as far as the circumstances go. The factors that combined to create the right conditions for an affair were: (a) the absence of a joint household with several members and the nuclear household with practically no restriction or diversion around; (b) the setting of the place, away from the fold of Bengali society, with the absence even of neighbors; (c) the personality of the *debar* with experience in a foreign land where free mixing between the sexes is natural; (d) the loneliness and the lack of occupation of the *boudi*, who was drawn easily to the interesting *debar*; (e) the indifference and tolerance of the husband whose trust and love for his brother allowed the situation to continue.

All these factors contribute toward the development of such an affair. But given them all, a sexual affair may not develop because of personalities. However, the circumstances are usually to the contrary in the section of Bengali society I am dealing with, and there the relationship hardly ever takes such a turn. In fact, from the *boudi's* point of view, it is more effective not to have a sexual affair. It gives her enough emotional satisfaction if she can reap the pleasure of a mixed relationship where the affective quality is strong (affection, love, friendship). On the other hand, an overt sexual affair, though it may be more intense, will create problems for both the partners and for their family, and they do not consider it worthwhile. The result, in that case, is more frustrating than satisfactory, especially since marriages are not dissolved to replace one of the partners in this culture.

Let me give one more representative example.

Case no. 28: I was very pleased to discover that I had a bunch of *debars* when I got married. My older sister, who was married two years before, often talked about her favorite *debar*, her husband's first cousin. It sounded like great fun. I even felt like suggesting to my sister to start a proposal of marriage between her *debar* and myself. From her description he sounded as if he was cut out to be

the perfect husband. Later, I realized that a *debar* is more fun
because he is a *debar*. At any rate, my own *debars* turned out to
be all great admirers of me. They competed with one another for
my favor and attention. I was offered gifts and the opportunity to
be taken out constantly by one or the other. Two of them even
declared that they would never get married unless the family
found them brides modeled after me. I was so grateful they
existed and helped me in all sorts of ways. It flattered me
immensely to have them around who adored me so much. My
favorite one was my husband's second cousin, who stayed in the
family and went to college in Calcutta. Where his parents lived
there was no good college. This *debar* was relatively shy and
reserved with others but talked a lot to me. He told me all his
secrets—problems with his parents and friends; he knew I would
never tell anyone. He liked to be with me alone and would be
quite overwhelmed when I accepted an invitation to go to a
movie with him. I enjoyed his rapt attention toward me. . . .
When I left Calcutta to join my husband in Delhi for six months,
he wrote me letters every other day. They were like love letters.
But I must admit I expected something like this and looked
forward to his letters because there was not much to do in Delhi.
Those letters gave me a lot of pleasure. This *debar* of mine left
our family after he finished his M.A. to take up a teaching
position in a small town. He wept when he told me this and felt
very sad to leave me. I myself felt terribly lonely and empty when
he left. My other *debars* were not quite the same to me. It took
me nearly a year to get over this pain of separation. Later I heard
he got married. I was curious to find out if his wife had any
similarities to me. Did he love his wife as much as he loved me?

The second type of role that the woman resorts to, and in
which she perhaps receives a longer lasting satisfaction, is the role
of "mother." Her frustrations in the relationship with her husband and the problems of adjustment to the *sasur-bāri* in general
push her into the fantasy of becoming a mother. The desire to
become a mother, however, is deep-seated in any woman,
irrespective of the circumstances. She has learned in the very
early years of her life that one of the most important roles of a
woman is to become a mother. Like marriage, this is the ultimate
destiny and fortune of every woman. If a woman is not blessed
with a child she is most unfortunate. During her first few years of

marriage, which offer her enough frustrations and loneliness, she sees the validity of this idea. She sees that the only tangible and long-lasting relationship is the one between mother and son. She sees how much time and affection her husband still has for his old mother. Besides, being a mother also allows her to attain status in the family and society. She becomes respectable overnight, so to speak. From the father-in-law to the maid, all begin to respect her when she is a mother. Even as a pregnant woman she captures attention and receives care from everyone including her husband. Her fear about pregnancy (from all the old wives' tales she has been hearing since childhood) is overcome by the benefits she can foresee in it. Also, she knows that if she does not bear a son soon she will lose prestige in all quarters. She may have more pressure on this matter, particularly if her husband happens to be the oldest son in the family. She must provide the family with a descendant. On her part, she herself would like to have a child very soon, particularly if she does not have *debars* (or *debar* figures) to divert her or children in the house requiring her attention. At any rate, her desire to become a mother is very strong although the expectations are still very vague. She is not quite sure what exactly she will feel and gain. She knows she will find in this highly prestigious role some sort of gratification in her marriage. This is not exclusive of her relationship with her *debar*; in fact, they are complementary. Thus she prepares herself to step into the mother's role, the ultimate achievement of a woman's life.

This reasoning may not be very conscious. She may just become pregnant and rationalize along this line. In most households like this, women practice birth control only very superficially, using the rhythm method. Her chances of becoming pregnant within a year of marriage are quite high, and once it happens she welcomes it. There is no strong deterrent against getting pregnant, as is very clear. Once pregnant, she sees the changes not only in her body and mind, but also in the attitudes of the people around her. From their suddenly increased attention she feels very important and wanted. She attains a special status as she did during the week of her wedding. This improves her self-image a great deal. She feels happy despite the physical discomfort and the worries that go with it. A sense of achievement creeps into her and everybody confirms it. Her husband not only becomes more attentive but also begins to show respect and some overt affection. He appears to be more comfortable with her; he can place her and knows how to treat her. He also sees the justification for their sexual relationship; it was not all for "pleasure," something he should not look for from his wife. The confirmation of the wife's fecundity relieves all the members of the family because at last the recruitment of the new woman in the family becomes justified.

Let's look into the husband's reactions more closely. It is clear that he feels somewhat uncomfortable with his wife until she shows signs of pregnancy. The relationship between them until that time remains amorphous and undefined. The social restrictions that are imposed on his free mixing with his wife, at the same time that she is the only available sexual partner, make the situation rather uncomfortable for him. He has also been socialized by the dictum that "A wife is needed to beget a son" and sexual union with her has no other purpose but to have a son. Therefore, if the period before pregnancy is prolonged he cannot help feeling embarrassed. His wife's expectation of romantic love mingled with sexual pleasure does not make sense to him, because he knows he is not supposed to enjoy sexual pleasure with his wife the way he can with a prostitute or a mistress. At the same time, his wife is the only woman at hand who wants and wishes to enjoy him. His understanding of things does not quite fit into this experience. The only way he can explain it to himself is that women in this society have more sexual desire than men do. His colleagues and friends with whom he discusses such topics all testify to this conclusion. This sexual ambivalence that a husband has toward his wife is very deep-rooted in the psychology and personality structure of Bengali men.

In order to understand this we have to go a bit deeper into both the sociocultural and religio-ideological history of Bengal. The premedieval literature abounds in evidences of the Hindu attitude toward women, which included a very frank acceptance of the flesh and sensual pleasure. The Vedic and epic gods, like the Greek and Roman deities, are a lecherous bunch constantly seducing the wives of sages and mortals. The sages and monks, surprisingly enough, are also depicted indulging in active sexual pleasure even though living as hermits. This era was followed by Brahmanical puritanism when sexual pleasure had to be subsumed under the rationale of the act of procreation—the supreme motive of sex—and this eventually gave rise to the concept of conjugal devotion. This is the only way the Bengalis could handle the situation, i.e., by separating sexual pleasure from marriage. To keep such enjoyment alive they had to adopt variations such as polygamy and prostitution. Both these institutions had definite economic disadvantages. Gradually such habits evolved into sporadic, sneaking affairs with available partners mostly recruited from among helpless widowed relatives or low-caste maids serving in the household. During the nineteenth century the sexual relationship between a man and a woman had three possible forms: [9] (1) one's own wife (shiyā); (2) others' wives (parakiyā); and (3) ordinary prostitutes (sāmanya banitā).

All three forms of relationship could be practiced simultaneously by the same person. However, by the end of the nineteenth century, with the abolition of polygamy and landlordism (associated with a feudal culture that openly encouraged prostitution), Bengali men had to resort to the second category only, which in reality meant nothing but sexual exploitation of helpless widows and lower-caste women. In the first relationship it was considered a duty for the husband to indulge in sex with his wife not for pleasure but to beget descendants. The other two relationships were complementary to the first. The relationship between husband and wife could sometimes grow into an affectionate one, but more often than not it was based on indifference on the husband's part and a grudging attitude of martyrdom on the part of the wife. Wives not only accepted their husbands' extramarital liaisons, they often provided the source of income for such adventures by selling their own jewelry because they had no alternatives. [10]

Such attitudes toward women and sex have been handed down to modern generations to a great extent. My data, though they do not cover many men as informants, indicate glimpses of such attitudes in at least one case study I described in a previous chapter. This shows clearly how young men, even today, view women, including their wives, and sexual relationships with them.

It seems Bengali culture has not been able to accept sexual pleasure (*kām*) in conjugal as well as romantic love. The dichotomy that men in many cultures are more or less indoctrinated with is emphasized more in Bengal (and perhaps all over India among the upper class and caste) because of this historical development of the attitude toward women since rather early in history. Part of the reasons of such indoctrination is, of course, the strong emphasis on respect for women—the mothers, the only category a Bengali man is associated with until his late adolescence. In his adolescence his exposure to sexual learning comes through his male friends along with the illustrated pornography he has access to, and they teach him that sexual pleasure (*kām*) is acceptable only with a woman he can desire. He does not learn to consider sexual pleasure as being natural and to be associated with the women he learned to respect until he begins to be influenced by the notion of romantic love between a married couple. However, the notion of romantic love for a man in marriage takes another interesting turn because of the persisting socialization within Bengali families along with the commercialization of romantic love achieved by the modern mass media.

This conflict in attitude toward women is reflected in the dichotomous image of two kinds of women—the mother (to be respected) and the mistress (to be desired sexually), and is illustrated in both ancient and modern literature despite a few sporadic attempts to incorporate the two into one image as Tagore attempted in some of his novels (see the chapter "Childhood and Adolescence").

This conflicting attitude toward sexual pleasure that women symbolize has its roots in most religious and mythological ideology. While sexual pleasure is most desirable, it is also felt to be most destructive to a man's physical and spiritual well-being. The two epics, *The Rāmāyana* and *The Mahābhārata*, are full of episodes in which the ascetic is seduced by a temptress, a woman who can allow him to experience pleasure and yet be free to go back to his *tapa* (meditation). Yet the whole mythology of Śiva (as interpreted in *Śiva-Purāna*) repeats the theme of his wife Pārvati's desperate attempt to divert him from his *tapa* and toward life, herself, and desire (*kāma*). Women are powerful, seductive, and destructive. [11]

As G. Morris Carstairs (1956, 1964) [12] observes among his

high-caste Rajput informants, Bengali men also, on the plane of creative fantasy, worship the goddess Durgā, on whom a man depends entirely for his protection, strength, and nurturance; but Durgā also has the aspect of Kāli, who is naked, black, angry, and destructive. She kills men and drinks their blood and wears a necklace made of their skulls; she dances on the prostrate body of her husband Śiva. Kāli, who is especially popular in Bengal, may be said to depict the negative and seductive as well as destructive side of women; she is a figure of adoration as well as fear.

In reality in this culture, a man from early childhood till adolescence has the unwavering assurance of his mother's love, affection, protection, and nurturance. The split image of Durgā and Kāli in religious fantasy does not seem to create confusion in real life because a Bengali man views his mother as entirely separate from the other kind of women, the destructive temptress, while he continues to worship both Durgā and Kāli as mother figures.

Throughout his life, the Bengali man's relationship with his nearest female blood relatives—his mother, sister, daughter— offers him the same protection and nurturance in bits and pieces. He has no difficulty relating to them all as parts of the "mother"— the Durgā image. The only two women who come to his life from outside are his wife and his brother's wife, and they pose some problems because with his wife he must relate sexually. With his sister-in-law the relationship, though it hardly becomes sexual due to the familial circumstances, evolves into a romantically close relationship. As for his wife, the cultural ideal of conjugal love does not permit him to treat her as a desired, fearful temptress figure. In fact, culture stresses the mother figure for the wife and the sister-in-law alike. In reality, the only way he can relate to his wife is by thinking of her as the Kāli aspect of the mother, because she is the only woman within the family available for sexual pleasure. But, as mentioned above, according to familial, social, and cultural ideology, she must be respected and treated as in the same category as the goddess-mother. Hence there results a lifelong confusion and ambivalence over a man's sexual relations with his wife. This state of confusion is further aggravated by the social custom of having no opportunity to build a close, warm relationship with his wife, as described earlier in this chapter. His handling of the situation is made less difficult by projecting the ascetic image of Śiva as the ideal husband. He becomes distant, indifferent, and withdrawn in relation to his wife. From the wife's point of view this may often be interpreted as being the self-centeredness of a husband who does not demonstrate love and affection for his wife. Śiva's asceticism is also said to enhance the power of fertility, because Hindu mythology emphasizes that it is necessary to amass the power of fertility by the practice of chastity and meditation. Śiva was also the master of the method (*yoga*) by which the virile force may be sublimated and transformed into a mental force, an intellectual power. Śiva was the great *yogi*. Every Hindu man, therefore, has this attitude toward retaining semen, symbol of virility, which is wasted if he often has sexual intercourse.

Thus the factors responsible for the impossibility of the development of a romantic love relationship (where the sexual act cannot be justified) between husband and wife are as follows. The dichotomous religious ideology a man internalizes is in the form of Durgā and Kāli, which in real life he can project only as two separate figures. Due to the pressure of social custom he has to treat his wife in the category of Durgā, even though he has to relate to her partly as Kāli (sex object). By treating all the women in the family in the same category his emotional security is insured. While his very close physical and emotional relationship with his mother in his childhood does not offer him total satisfaction in adult life, his wife offers the sexual part and his sister-in-law the friendship. But sexual pleasure is never complete because of the conflict in the image. Therefore, the sexual desire may remain unfulfilled all his life unless he has extramarital affairs with such women as prostitutes. [13]

Going back to the newly acquired motherhood of the woman, once the child is born she shifts her total attention to the child and the family also shifts its attention to the child. Except for a few days following delivery, the new mother does not require physical attention to a great extent. She may spend a couple of months around the time of childbirth in her natal home. But this custom is not so strictly followed in this section of the society as among the middle- and lower middle-class and rural people. At any rate, her absorption with her child, whom she learns to love, is total, even though the caring and rearing of the child may be shared by all the women in the household. The mother breast-feeds him, sleeps with him in the same bed (which the husband may also share), dresses him, bathes him, and sings songs to him to put him to sleep. Everybody constantly tells her how fortunate she is having a son, and she must work very hard and love him very much to keep this treasure she has got through such physical pain. This is a gift every woman aspires to have and lives for. This is why she has been married in the first place. Thus, the mother totally escapes into her newly found role for a while and tries to feel elated, honored, and proud because everybody around her believes she does. She may continue to be absorbed in her children for the next ten years or so if she continues to produce a child every other year or even more frequently. However, this absorption is never complete. The aura of motherhood, like everything else, also wears off after a while. Her very close attachment to her son makes her weary and very dependent. She begins to worry about losing him when he grows up. Meanwhile she also begins to see that the expectations she has had about marriage and her husband cannot be compensated for by the role of mother alone.

She continues to remain close to her brother-in-law. But neither of the involvements can be complete. She cannot possibly have much time for her *debar*, and she feels guilty about her duties toward her children if she does not pay total attention to them. To be a mother, as she knows and hears from all directions, is not a joking matter.[14] It requires a great deal of sacrifice. She tries to feel satisfied by glorifying this idea to herself. The glorification of the mother image that the classics and modern literature, as well as the mass media, constantly amplify also helps her reinforce the belief. But she knows from direct experience that the ideal depicted by all literature is never realized in life. She is still not sure if other women go through the same disillusionment. It seems as if the older women in the family are doing fairly well. No one talks about it. She herself is not sure how to express it either. She knows this much: that things did not go quite right. She knows, for example, the satisfaction she enjoyed with her relationship with the *debars* was not quite what she anticipated or planned. The desire to have a child and to become a mother, after it is done, does not seem to be so great an achievement after all. She misses the days when she was full of dreams and expectations about her future, when she giggled for hours, weaving dreams with her friends about their future husbands and lovers!

Her father, who was so great a friend, philosopher, and guide to her, never disappointed her. At least that's what she thinks now, looking back to those carefree, happy days.

These thoughts are not always well formulated in the minds of the women. I happened to have one very articulate informant who put it very nicely.

Case no. 29: I am beginning to think at this age of forty that something must be wrong with life itself. We plan to be happy and do all sorts of things that our mothers and grandmothers and our fathers taught us. I tried my best to please my husband the way he wanted me to behave. I also tried all the ideal behavior a daughter-in-law is expected to act out. I enjoyed doing it most of the time, but often I felt tired and did not see much point in anything. When my first son was born I was very happy for several months. But then I developed this infection and often cursed him out of pain. If I had not had him perhaps I never would have had the infection. I also found out very soon that my son, no matter how much he loved me, would go away someday and would love his wife. This is the way life is. But this knowledge could not make me accept it totally. I am often convinced that we women are born to suffer. And if I, like my grandmother, could believe in this totally, I could perhaps accept my life a lot easier. But I learned to read other kinds of things where people talk about other kinds of life and women do not seem to suffer everywhere. Or maybe they do. What do you think? You have traveled in many countries. Do you know if women in any country in this world feel happy about their life?

At this stage she again tries to seek satisfaction through other available roles. The next chapter elaborates on the woman's last phase of her life after she ceases to give birth and begins to feel unhappy at being old and unwanted.

4 Later Years and Old Age

Having a child, no matter at what age, changes the status of a woman in all classes of Indian society, including upper-class Bengal. Becoming a mother, in fact, is not so much a change of status as it is the attainment of the status a woman is born to achieve. No woman is more unfortunate than one who is unable to bear a child.

In this section of Bengali society the ideal of ultimate motherhood, though tacitly assumed, is not overplayed, but a woman is subtly made to feel her misfortune by her family, neighbors, and relatives if she does not become a mother within two to five years after her marriage. She becomes a mother (*mā*) and continues to be one till she stops reproducing, at which stage she becomes the matron-mother (*ginni-mā*) of the family and often of the neighborhood. Let us turn then to this phase of a woman's life, the last phase and a very crucial one in terms of her psychological frustrations and the compensatory gratifications she is allowed to choose. It follows immediately after the biologically most productive and respectable stage a woman can reach. The physiopsychological contrast between her most productive fifteen to twenty years of married life and the unproductive twenty to twenty-five years thereafter is a very significant one as it is all over the world. In Bengali society, attempts are made to underplay such physiopsychological transitions by extending the recognition of motherhood (and the respect associated with it) to the woman beyond her reproductive age. She not only remains a mother (*mā*) to her children, daughters-in-law, sons-in-law, and the servants, she also becomes the *ginni-mā*, the matron-mother, a status that indicates the climax of a woman's life. Now she is important in her own standing; she has gone through her times of adjustment, disillusionment, and illusion. She has served and obeyed the elders; it's now her turn to be listened to and respected by all, including the men in the house. The image of a *ginni-mā* is so clearly emphasized by this culture that every member of the society has a visual picture of such a respectable woman. She is between forty-five and fifty-five years of age, somewhat plump from years of childbearing and eating predominantly starchy foods, without much physical exercise; she wears a white sari with a red border and vermilion on her forehead, and the parting of her hair (the sign of marriage in Bengal) is equally red; she has a bunch of keys on a ring tied at the end of her sari that also covers her head; her mouth, like her sari-border, is red from chewing betel-leaf and nut with lime. This image, which is very clear-cut in everybody's mind, is quite symbolic. The red in her hair, forehead, and the sari-border indicates her fortunate status in being married and not yet a widow. She is very proud of the broad stain on the parting of her hair that the powder of the vermilion has left after constant use every day for years, for this indicates that she is happy because she has a husband. Her plump and somewhat loose body indicates the years of childbearing and prosperous living, as opposed to young women who are slim. She is no longer a woman who can be looked at with desire or pity, but she must be respected. The keys that open and lock several rooms including the kitchen, the pantry, and the storeroom symbolize her command and authority in the household—something her mother-in-law and older sister-in-law once enjoyed.

When she was first married she had a great many romantic expectations that were triggered by her experience of erotic love. Now she is ending her sexual experience with the associated feeling of losing not only her youth, but also the attention paid to a woman who is desired and loved, rather than one who is respected and, sometimes, deified. In spite of the emphasis the society puts on her role as matron-mother, her personal, emotional, and sexual satisfaction from this role is by no means total. Her interactions with her husband and other members of the family at this stage fail to compensate for her emotional and sexual frustrations.

Interaction with the Husband

Since the time of her first child, her relationship with her husband has changed to some extent. It has become more relaxed and informal. The husband finds it easier to relate to her, now that she has become a mother. During the subsequent years when they have other children, the sexual relationship does not create much embarrassment for him because now he can justify it as an instrument of reproduction. She becomes so involved with her children and in the rearing of them that she learns to live with her husband's attitude. By the time she has had her fourth or fifth child, even if they are spaced more than two years apart, she may still be in her late thirties. In other words, she may still be sexually active and able to reproduce. Unless she has eight to ten children, which is not the norm in this section of society, she will not be busy reproducing up to the time of menopause. In the absence of any numerical data on this, one can only hazard guesses from observation. I have no definite indication of conscious birth-control measures that either of the partners take to increase the spacing or to limit the number of offspring. The control is achieved indirectly by automatic abstention due to the postpartum sex taboo: physical separation when the wife returns to her family home for several months after delivery, plus other kinds of ritual abstention. [1]

Be that as it may, a woman in this culture is not encouraged to bear more than five or six children. The sanction against a woman having too many is based not on any rational grounds such as economic conditions, but more as a status distinction from her fecund and uneducated rural counterpart. Also, since education, especially higher education for the male children, is very highly valued, the size of the family is kept smaller so that the financing of their education and the weddings of the daughters are not difficult. Consequently, a woman may stop reproducing before she is even close to the age of menopause. But after her last child she is made to believe by society that she is entering the time of waning sexual and reproductive capacity, even though in reality she may not be. If she has her last child in her mid-thirties, she may only remain absorbed in rearing it till she is forty. In this respect, the Bengali proverb "A woman is old by the time she is twenty" has some truth in it.

The husband-wife relationship, as already indicated, begins to change with the birth of the first child. The husband may even demonstrate some overt affection and attention toward his wife, because she is not simply his wife but his child's mother. This attention is easy for him to offer because it is the same quality of attention the rest of the family is offering too. He begins to address his wife in the same way the older relatives in the family do: "The mother of the baby" or "The mother of so-and-so." Her identity now becomes that of "mother of her child." At any rate, the affection that grows between the husband and his child's mother is often a strong one and may represent the ideal of conjugal love (devoid of the romantic and erotic content) that the texts, both religious and secular, emphasize. [2] I would like to give one example of such conjugal love, the main content of which is affection on the one hand and respect on the other, rather than erotic love between equals. The nature of such idealized conjugal love was expressed very well in a little book written by a Bengali husband, a well-known academician from upper middle-class Calcutta, after his wife's death at the age of sixty-five. The obituary was written in memory of his wife and their fifty years of married life. It is interesting that despite his exposure to western education and contact through many travels and lecture tours, this man believed so strongly in the Hindu ideal of a wife. The excerpts below will substantiate this. [3]

My wife passed away with most of her wishes fulfilled as a Hindu woman. She saw her daughters married and well-established in life. Her only son had a good college career, and she had selected his bride, and her son got his special training in America, and was in a good post in a technical and industrial firm. She was quite happy and proud of her position in life, with a husband and a son upon whom she doted and on whom she could also rely, and with five daughters who were happily married, and her five sons-in-law who were just like her own sons, and her daughters' children who were her loving grandchildren.... The Sanskrit adage says that the wife is the Home, and the ideal wife has been characterized by the ancient Indian poet Kalidasa as the Mistress of the House, Adviser and Manager of Affairs, Trusted Friend as well as Beloved Pupil in the Fine Arts.... My wife, indeed, was permeating every part of our house.... She appreciated the value of the work that I was doing, and with her it was her first charge to see that I could carry on my appointed tasks to the best of my ability ... My wife, born to the tradition [of joint-family living], accepted it as a matter of course and she went on for any amount of sacrifice and self-abnegation, more than myself. My wife herself was a God-fearing woman, with faith and piety in the traditional Hindu way, like most of us. She believed in the rites and rituals of Hindu domestic life and worship, and herself performed them carefully.... She was very much in love with life, and yet she often manifested in her behavior a strange detachment and objectivity which we frequently see in our Indian womanhood.

For some years after our marriage, there was in me a sense of pride and happiness in having the love and complete abandon and the absolute reliance on me of a young woman whose very life was centered in me. But as the years passed, this deepened into something wider and far more profound—a sense of perfect understanding of each other's mind and personality.

These excerpts, written in English for distribution among his friends and relatives in both India and abroad, show how a husband views, or perhaps more realistically, is supposed to view, his wife's role in his life and his family. This appears to be in perfect accord with the ideal presented and stressed by the early Sanskrit texts and by folk beliefs. What is significant is not whether the evaluation of his wife is correct, but the idea that the feelings of a grieving husband are well expressed through such recollections and evaluations of his wife's qualities, which appear to be near-perfect according to the cultural ideal. This is what all husbands in their later years are expected to feel and believe because otherwise their married lives would be considered unfulfilled, imperfect, and therefore unhappy. In a marriage where dissolution is not socially permitted, except for disguised desertion due to barrenness, a life together within the joint-family, despite unhappiness, may develop into an understanding based on a mixture of illusion and reality—the ideals one is expected to achieve and wants to achieve. As the members of a joint-family, it is convenient for a couple in their late fifties and sixties to imagine and even make believe that they have had a fulfilled and, therefore, happy married life. What constitutes this fulfillment is expressed above.

As we move from ideology to real life, the picture may not always be perfect because the wife who is approaching middle age after years of frustrations may not experience the ideal conditions the gentleman in his obituary makes us believe his wife had. Let us take another case, which may be considered more or less typical.

As mentioned before, the woman may be in her early forties by the time her engrossing involvement with her last child is over. At this time, if her first child is a girl, she may feel quite conscious of her role as a responsible mother and may look into, or at least think of, her daughter's marriage. She also joins the older women in looking after and doing things for others, such as her children, relatives, and so on. She is almost forced to play this role because if she does not, her frustrations from adverse familial opinion and her own loneliness can be very acute. She must not expect much for herself. The husband, of course, shows respect and affection, but the sense of failure their relationship has had for her, because of her disappointment in romantic love, is still there (see chap. 3); her increased interaction with him in everyday life does not alter this. She may spend more time talking to him about the children or the other members of the family, and he may pay more heed than before. They may even become allies against a brother who is a burden on the family or a sister-in-law who is partial to her own children. The husband may even pay more attention to her counseling in certain matters. But because he rarely paid attention to her wisdom in the early stages of their marriage, she knows that this attention is due to her age and position in the family, not to her own worth. After fifteen or twenty years of married life, she has learned to live with a husband who has never quite fulfilled her expectations of the rich love and friendship talked about in books. He is merely falling into the pattern of his father and forefathers of granting his wife, who bore his family descendants and provided services to himself, her due. The relationship is adjusted, and perhaps well-adjusted, between the role of "the husband" and the role of "the wife" rather than between two human beings. They have learned to accept each other's needs, characters, hopes, aspirations, and faults, but they do not meet on common ground. Since the husband was never taught to believe in such communication, he may not even know about his wife's frustrations. Since the wife has had mixed training, feeding her romantic expectations, even though she may not be able to verbalize her needs, she knows and feels what she has received and what she has settled for. She has reached the stage where she does not hope for any qualitative change in their relationship. She accepts this as a matter of fact in everyday life. However, she tries to find satisfaction for her personal needs elsewhere, as she always has.

Her sex life with her husband at this stage becomes very irregular and gradually may stop well before she is fifty, because as it was before she first became pregnant, sexual contact with her husband again becomes embarrassing. It is considered unbecoming, and almost unnatural, to engage in such pleasures at their age, after the need for having children is over. The sleeping arrangement also is inconvenient. Since the family does not approve of such an act, the woman is expected to sleep with her children or other older women. During the first few years of marriage, even though the bed is shared by the children, usually only the very young sleep with them so that the intimacy for the couple is not as difficult. Even if the couple continues to sleep in the same room, it is very unlikely that they sleep alone. Her own or a sister-in-law's children usually share the bed with them. A subtle social stigma is attached to the habit of sharing the same bed with her husband when her children are grown. This is often expressed in casual conversations among the women of the household. A mother is not only not supposed to sleep with her husband, but also is expected to dress and behave rather conservatively when her son is grown. She should not wear any color other than white, and she must not pay too much attention to her physical adornment. It does not become her to adorn herself because she is beyond the desire and lust of men. She is as pure as the white of her sari, and this image is very important for her, and especially for her growing son, who soon learns how to distinguish between a woman who is unrespectable because she is desirable and women who belong to the category of "mother." The common expressions criticizing a woman with grown children who may dress a bit attentively may be: "How can she dress like a young thing when she has sons old enough to be fathers themselves? Does she not have any shame?" Or, "What will my son think if I dress like a young woman?" Or, "Why should I wear jewelry? My sons are my jewelry."

Thus her sexual needs are totally underplayed as she stops bearing children. This is not to claim that some couples do not continue to have sex. But most do not because of the subtle but often quite overt familial and social sanctions against it.

Interaction with Sons and Daughters

From about her early forties, a woman's involvement with her children is no longer of an engrossing physical kind. They are grown and have become physically independent. Her relationship with her daughters is one of authority and covert affection. If she still has young, unmarried daughters, it is also tinted with tension because of the close father-daughter contact (see chap. 1). She knows all about it because she has been a daughter once herself. But the knowledge is somewhat slanted now, the angle has changed. In other words, the understanding is not enough to take away the tension that the daughter's existence creates between the husband and wife. Her son is her only salvation. The involvement that she began to build up since the day he was born has been growing deeper everyday. Now he is grown and soon may go away to study, work, and to be married eventually. Though the decline of the son's need for motherly love is imminent, the mother does not know how to tolerate this. Or rather, she does not allow herself to see the reality. In this society a mother is not made to realize this. She knows that her greatest achievement as a woman is in having a son and all the social customs and beliefs reinforce the fact that this is the source of ultimate happiness and value. She is never told that she will have to part with this happiness sooner or later. The fact that her son, who has been the center of her world until he is grown, does not depend on her as much as he did when he was young is very hard for her to accept. She understands that he is an adult and must find his way around the world, but she does not understand and cannot accept why he has to get away from her all-engrossing love and attention. Despite all the facts of life to the contrary, in this culture neither the mother nor the son ever believes in this separation. She knows that he has to associate with others and eventually he must marry another woman. The son, from his point of view, sees the predicament of having a mother who is his first responsibility and obligation, but also a strong source of emotional security. But he must get away from her without inflicting pain. He knows that he should prepare to give himself and be close to another woman—his wife. But he does not have the courage to give up the security of his mother's love, which, due to the custom of living together, is always there. Consequently, his romantic relationship with his wife never takes on a real form, and he continues to wait until he is able to treat her as the mother of his child. On the other hand, despite the physical separation, he knows that his mother is never going to leave him or withdraw her love from him. This confidence that he is made to believe in by all socializing methods not only makes him take his mother for granted but also interferes with his love-relationship with his wife. Besides, from the viewpoint of society he is not expected to have a total love-relationship with his wife, anyway. But his mother, in whom her son has such confidence, feels neglected nevertheless, because he is not always physically there to satisfy her and express his appreciation. When a society emphasizes and idealizes the mother-son relationship, the idea becomes almost abstract and the responsibility to keep it alive tends to decrease. A mother's love is taken for granted, so the son does not need to work hard to nourish it. He only needs to be ready to accept it. The mother, who has been disappointed in her relationship with her husband and who is allowed by the family and society to devote herself totally to her son, perhaps expects more than would a mother in another culture. At the age of forty or fifty her fear of losing her son's undivided attention is most acute. She has no identity apart from this. At the same time, she is not allowed to continuously enjoy emotional fulfillment from it, despite all the external labeling and adornment that society offers her as a mother.

Thus the satisfaction that she derived when she gave birth to a son and the satisfaction she continued to derive by giving the child her complete affection and attention now is on the wane because she expects the same in return. She realizes that as a mother all she can expect to receive from those around her is respect for her self-sacrificing love that gives the son security forever, but does not demand anything in return. This quality of motherhood is well known to her, but the knowledge does not minimize her frustrations. Her son returns her love to some extent, in the sense that he is there to receive it. But she is weary and tired of all the giving; she needs some care and attention in return. The attention and respect as well as the care she receives from the family do not give her the emotional satisfaction that she hoped to have from her husband, her husband's brothers, and now from her son. One case that I observed is relevant in this context.

Case no. 30: There was a family with three sons and three daughters, who were married and away. The oldest son was away in England studying medicine. The second son, who was twenty-five, finished college and spent time developing various hobbies such as performing in musical groups, amateur acting, and so on. The youngest son was still at high school. The father, who was in his early sixties, had enough property in terms of land and small business. The family was quite secure economically. The second son, who was very close to his mother [who was about fifty] not only spent quite a bit of time chatting with her but also remained close physically. I was surprised to watch him come home late in the evening from his music rehearsals and hug the mother like a child, pressing his face to her breasts. He would often find her in bed resting and would place his own body very close to hers, pressing his palms loosely on her breasts as babies do. This was done regularly, with little self-consciousness. At night he slept in a separate room, but during the day he would lie down next to his mother off and on whenever she took her midafternoon nap. Often the discussion of his marriage would come up (his elder brother decided not to marry), and he would say that he did not need a wife so long as his mother was alive. Besides, as he put it, he did not wish to risk his mother's happiness by marrying an unknown woman who might turn out to be mean and quarrelsome. He could not do that to this mother; he was not like his elder brother who was selfish to be away and looking only after his career. His mother, on the other hand, tried to talk him into a marriage with the argument that she was getting old and she needed a young woman to help her with the housework. Besides, she needed grandchildren to keep herself happy in her declining years. But I noticed how proud and happy she looked because she had such a devoted son who was tied to her sari, so to speak. So far as I know the young man did not get married even after two more years. When and if he gets married the likelihood of conflict and tension between the mother-in-law and the daughter-in-law will be very great.

The case above is, however, not a very typical one. Usually, the son in his adolescent years becomes attached to a sister-in-law or, if he has none, a substitute such as a friend's sister-in-law may attract his attention. In other words, he does not need to be around his mother; he needs a younger woman to understand him and give him friendship (see the previous chapter). So even before the son is married the mother may begin to lose him, although certain prerogatives still belong to her as a mother. For example, she may supervise his meals and attend to him when he is sick. But the communication on an emotional level is reduced to a great degree because he has less time for her.

Interaction with Brother-in-law

Her other close relation, the brother-in-law (*debar*) who saved her from her frustrations at the very beginning of her married life, also has less time for her now. He may be married and for several months quite intrigued by his new wife. He still keeps close contact with his favorite *boudi* and lets her take care of some of his needs, but it is clear that he does not need her as he did ten years ago. During this period the sister-in-law (*boudi*) herself has been bearing and rearing children, and the *debar* gradually became a bit distant and perhaps has found companionship elsewhere—with a younger sister-in-law perhaps. He does not treat her as a friend anymore, but with respect as do others in the family. The personal bond they had between them has been buried with time. She can also feel a tension because she knows from her own experience that he must show more attention to his wife than to her. Besides, she is older, not young and attractive as she was ten years ago. In her position as a *ginni-mā* (matron-mother) she should outgrow such a need as a young man's companionship. Now her interaction with him may include a passing remark or two or perhaps a chat after dinner when the conversation remains superficial. She is expected to joke about his new married life, and understandably she has a hard time doing so. She cannot help feeling a pang of jealousy, unless the *debar* decides to remain as close as before, in which case the situation may get quite out of hand and evoke strong criticism from the family.

Her daughters, who have been married or soon will be married, are not part of the family. Her sons, if they are marriageable, may not be married or may have no children yet, thus preventing her from becoming a full-fledged grandmother.

Thus, a woman of this age suddenly feels alone and abandoned in spite of her ascribed status as "*ginni-mā*," matron-mother. For partial gratification of her emotional and sexual frustrations, she usually has a number of alternatives, depending on a combination of circumstances.

One, she may plunge completely into the household if she happens to be the oldest daughter-in-law and her mother-in-law is either dead or unable to take on the responsibilities of the household. This may keep her somewhat engaged, but since in these households she usually has servants and maids to help her, the involvement in the house is never total and all-engaging. To compensate for this she may become a figure of power and authority and the matron-mother turns into a matriarch. This may happen only if she already has a temperament for such a role and she faces enough challenges in the household to become one. For example, she may have a model of a strong and powerful matriarch either in her own mother or in her mother-in-law, or the men in the household may not be efficient and authoritarian enough so that she needs to become one.

To my question how she felt about her life, one fifty-year-old woman told me the following:

Case no. 31: I have no time to think. You should see me through a typical day. I get up early in the morning and get busy looking after everybody's needs and comforts. Nothing seems to go on without me. I wonder what will happen to this family when I close my two eyes [meaning death]. Right now I do not even dare think of it. Even those stupid servants cannot move a finger without my instructions. God only knows what my reverend mother-in-law ever taught them. I cannot take a vacation, like all men do who work in offices. If I go away to see my old parents or somewhere else even for a week, the world falls apart. . . . Last year when my third sister got married I could not say "no" to my old parents who have been begging me to go and see them. They were a bit sore because in the last twenty years I could not get away from here to pay them a visit. They never seem to understand how tangled up I am in this family. Anyway, this time I was determined to take off and left for a week. It was a wonderful, relaxing vacation till I came back. Everything got out of hand. The kids got sick, the pantry had no supply of food, the men were in bad temper, two servants quit their jobs, one maid left, and all the rest of it. As if the whole household went crazy. I wonder what will happen to this family when I close my two eyes.

It is clear that she was enjoying the responsibility and the belief that the household could not function without her presence and competent supervision. This may be partly true, but old matrons like her exaggerate this fact to the extent that they live for this somewhat contrived satisfaction. In their actions they give the members of the family, as well as the neighbors, the impression of omnipotent presence. No one is able to ignore her. This power may sometimes (depending on the personality trend) be mingled with great capability and an affectionate nature, and may command not only authority but also respect and love. She may really become a *ginni-mā* in the fullest sense of the term. A woman who chooses to do so also extends her service and command beyond her joint-family. She may be equally feared and revered by the whole neighborhood. She may be depended on by the neighbors in case of illness, death, or any other kind of family crisis. She becomes the mother of and for the neighborhood, so to speak. This role and the successful carrying out of it brings a great deal of satisfaction to a woman at this stage of life.

The second alternative may be entirely different from the first, and a number of factors may combine to lead her to it. If the woman has had no children, or has had only one or two, thus leaving her without the engaging job of child-rearing before she is even thirty, if the household is small with fewer children and adults to look after, and if she happens to be of a temperament not suited to be a matriarch, she may very well choose to find a *guru*, a religious guide of some kind. When a woman does not have young children and is approaching middle age (in this culture between thirty and forty), she is encouraged to engage herself in full-time religious activities. Most households in this section of Bengali society have shrines where the older women daily offer flowers and food to the deities. In return the deities are expected to take care of the welfare of the family. The shrine also serves the purpose of a security spot for the women as well as the young. No member goes out of the house for any important job (exams, long journeys, interviews for jobs) without praying to the household deity. The rite of the daily offering is done usually by the old (post-menopause) and the very young (pre-menstruation). Apart from the fact that this is to avoid polluted women, the young girls also learn this duty of worshiping so that they will be able to continue it when they are old. The older women also usually become initiated by a *guru* (or a *sādhu-bābā* as he is called colloquially) who teach them particular chants that they repeat when they pray two or three times a day at the shrine. The idea is that she needs a guide to show her the path to reach her god. Some families may have lineage *gurus* (*kula-guru*) whose duty it is to initiate the older women in every generation. His son, who may become the next *kula-guru*, may continue doing so while enjoying the respect and maintenance of the disciples' family. Sometimes men in the household may also decide to be initiated by the *kula-guru*. The *kula-guru* may be approached for a number of other services such as reading the horoscopes of members in the family, especially before they are married or when they are ill. Some conservative families do not take any steps concerning serious matters (new business, marriage, sending boys for higher education) without the *kula-guru's* advice.

A woman who does not become a matriarch may decide to be

initiated by a *guru* early, because she feels this way she may overcome her frustrations and sense of being lonely. If she decides to do so she is very much encouraged by her family and the society. In the minds of her relatives, nothing can be better for a woman of her age to be preoccupied with. She may choose the *kula-guru* that her mother-in-law was initiated by or perhaps a new one.

This kind of *guru*, present in Bengal in great numbers (and to some extent in some other parts of India also), must not be confused with the classical *guru*—the teacher who trained the students in classical literature in their own homes or seminaries. The Indian education system, which has been highly influenced by the English method and content of teaching, is still predominantly based on such ideas as can be seen in the teacher-student relationship, for example. The *guru* a Bengali woman seeks in her later age is a man who is usually well-versed in Bengali religious literature (especially the Vaishnava literature) in which the love between a god and his worshipers is the major theme. He is a *guru* to the extent that he is supposed to teach her this technique of love to take her closer to her god. He also speaks well in local dialects and folk language (in everyday colloquialisms) that can capture the attention of uncultivated and less-educated women. He may be as young as forty or forty-five, and more often than not good-looking, judged by the standard of the culture he is dealing with. He wears expensive clothes (usually gifts from his rich disciples) and decorates himself with flowers, sandalwood paste, and perfumes, especially when he is in audience. The place where he receives his disciples and guests (would-be disciples) is charged with an atmosphere comparable to that of a Hindu temple. The aroma of flowers, incense, and sandalwood, along with religious chants and music, and disciples either sitting or prostrating themselves at the feet of the *guru* in near trances or hysteria, all give a very special atmosphere to the *guru* and his surroundings. He becomes a replica, a representative of the god. He treats his disciples on a very personal level; he calls them by their first names and often even nicknames. He gives patient hearing to their talk and confessions and advises with great sympathy. Often he does not give any advice, but just listens with sympathy and encouragement.

A woman who reaches the age of forty or so in the kind of

household described not only finds this as an escape from her family where she thinks she is not wanted anymore, but also finds someone to whom she can offer her love, affection, devotion, and respect. Her conscious rationale is: the *guru* is a representative of the god. She is giving to the god what she should give as a human being. For her emotional self, and this is usually unconscious, the *guru* may take the shape of a father whom she loved and adored in her childhood, a husband whom she expected to love and receive love from in her youth, and a brother-in-law and a son she is going to lose soon. And above all, the *guru* is the medium by which she can reach the god, the ultimate to which a mortal can aspire. The religious content that she was socialized to know as the underlying content of a husband-wife relationship (the model of Krishna and Rādhā as the acme of romantic as well as religious love) allows her to relate to her *guru* without any difficulty. She and others see no abnormality in such a relationship. On the contrary, this is the best thing she can do at this time of her life. She must give herself totally to the god in order to reach him and be blessed by him; and she has to do it with the help of a *guru*. [4]

Her husband may be the only man raising some objection, not in terms of her relationship with her *guru*, but for the fact that an involvement like this often takes a lot of her time and attention away from her family and especially from her husband. He also must feel jealous, no matter what religious rationale such involvement may have in the eyes of the people in the society. One husband told me the following:

Case no. 32: When she began to go to her *guru* along with the women in the neighborhood I did not mind. At the beginning she went once a week on Sundays and spent four to five hours there, God only knows doing what. Then gradually she began to go every other day and nowadays she goes every day. She also hid this from me because she was afraid I would disapprove. I found out about all this accidentally through a colleague of mine whose mother-in-law also visits the same *guru*. When I asked her she tried to lie. I could observe a kind of absentminded attitude in her; as if she does not enjoy doing housework anymore. As if she was not there. She told me at last that she had no attraction left for her *samsār* [family] and she would be very happy to be united with him, the god. I almost feel like going to this *guru* of hers and ask him why he was doing this to mislead housewives from their duties and responsibilities. I tell you I am quite upset about the whole business, but I cannot do anything about it.

The *guru* treats the woman like a child as well as a woman. He addresses her as a father does his daughter. She calls him *bābā*, the same term she uses for her father. He encourages her to tell him about her troubles, and she pours out her complaints against her husband, family, and all. Her need to depend and to be depended on seem to be most important for her at this age. The *guru* offers both. She feels the same security she did as a child with her father and enjoys the pleasure of the attention that a man can give a woman. If the *guru* is young and handsome, the pleasure and satisfaction are even more. Besides, unlike her husband and sons, the *guru* does not delude her. He is there to accept her offerings, her love. She cooks food and brings it to him; she offers flowers and food as a priest offers to the deity in the temple. Her human attraction for the *guru* is easily justifiable as a very strong pull mortals ought to have for the god. For the first time she can relate to a man of flesh and blood with the love and devotion she should offer the god. For the first time she realizes the intensity of the divine love that Rādhā must have felt for Krishna, even though physical union is not the rule in this case. In fact, the physical basis of this kind of total love is somewhat irrelevant, I think, although the woman may fantasize and get indirect sexual gratification by imagining herself as a lover of the *guru* as Rādhā was for Krishna. The need for such fantasies may be prominent in some cases where the woman may be young enough and has had very little sexual and emotional gratification from her marriage. But in the majority of the cases when a woman finds a *guru* she may be around or above fifty already and her experience with her husband for years has taught her to repress sexual desire quite effectively. She may not even have conscious need for it anymore. At any rate, the gratification she seeks and finds from her relationship with her *guru* is not directly based on sexual gratification. It is a total abandonment of giving herself with all the affective content of her feelings and desires that she has learned to give, but could not give totally because of the absence of recognition and response.

I have one interesting case that will demonstrate what I mean by the combination of factors leading to the *guru*-disciple relationship between a *guru* and a middle-aged Bengali woman.

Case no. 33: I met this woman at a funeral ceremony for a relative of hers in Calcutta. I had heard about her before. Many people talked about her devotion to religion. The woman was forty-five and still quite good-looking. To my query she related the following.

When I was married I was eighteen years old and found my *sasur-bāri* very different from my *baper-bāri* [father's household]. My husband, who is a businessman, often spent time away from home in connection with his business. I had no children and I became very lonely especially after most of my *nanads* [sisters-in-law] were married off. My mother-in-law died five years after my marriage, and the responsibility for the whole family fell on me. This kept me busy but I got tired of this responsibility; I always liked to read and be on my own. Even though I was lonely I enjoyed it. I read the epics several times, though I was not particularly religious-minded. During this time, that is two years ago, one afternoon a neighbor-woman asked me if I would like to go and visit the *bābā* [the *guru*] with her. He is supposed to be very famous and very kind. All women of the neighborhood wanted to be his disciples. I thought, why not? There were about a hundred people in a big room where he was sitting on a higher platform. I sat at a distance with my *sari* over my head and watched how people respected him and almost worshiped him. The room smelled of incense. I felt very drawn toward him. He was tall, thin, and handsome. I thought he also had a glow on his face, the kind of glow I saw on the faces of gods in the temples. I began to think how the god himself looked. Did he look like this *bābā*?

After about four or five hours, when many people left, someone came to me and said that the *bābā* wanted to see me. I was surprised and happy, I went to him and he got up and asked me to follow him. I followed him like in a dream walk. We passed through some hallways and went into a small room where only one earthen lamp was standing at the corner of the room. It was quite dark and cool. He closed the door behind him and asked me what I wanted. I said I did not know. I felt I would soon faint. I felt I was facing the god himself. I could say that I wanted to be his disciple, I wanted him to take me, guide me. I think I began to fall, because he held me and carried me to a soft bed. I do not remember anything after that. I felt very exalted and happy as if I was united with the god. After several hours I came round and felt very fatigued. I came home with the neighbor in a taxi and was in bed for several days afterward. Everybody thought I went through a great transformation. I became close to the god. After this experience I became the *bābā's* disciple. I could not think of anything but him—my god. My husband resented my new moods, and when I refused to sleep with him he was surprised and afraid. But knowing that I was determined to become religious and leave worldly pleasures, he kept quiet. Now I think he has become used to it. I suspect he even enjoys the fact that I am quite well known for my religious activities. He must be proud of the fact that *bābā* considers me as one of his best disciples. He honors our home by coming at least twice a year and gives me chances to serve and worship him.

Her words tell their own story, and many other women have similar stories to tell. Consider the following case, for example.

This woman is fifty-five and has seven children. Her husband is a retired lawyer and is ill with diabetes. Her mother-in-law is very old and is busy with her household deities. Her four daughters and two sons are all married. One son lives with them along with his new wife. The other son is away with his family in another city where he works. The third son is in Germany studying for a higher degree in philosophy. She has everything a woman of her background and age may hope to have (in terms of her cultural values). Yet, she was very restless and unhappy, until, as she told me, she found this *guru*. Her story is as follows:

Case no. 34: After my second son got married I hardly had much to do. His wife looked after his daily needs, and he spent a lot of time going out with her visiting friends and so on. My husband, who is in bed most of the time, is no good to talk to. All he had to say is how sick he was. My mother-in-law spends most of her days and nights in her *thākur ghar* [household shrine]. I got tired of waiting for everyone to get home for dinner and to wait upon my sick husband day and night. Suddenly I felt I was superfluous, not needed in my own household. My mother-in-law, who herself must have gone through the same feelings, one day suggested that I might consider seeing a *guru*. In fact she was willing to take me

to her own *guru*, who was also the *kula-guru*. But I did not like
her *guru* at all. I thought he was too thin and strange looking. As
a matter of fact I used to laugh at his picture when I first got
married. He is also very, very old. One of my cousin-sisters, who
lives in Bihar, once visited us and told me that she could ask her
guru to read my husband's horoscope to see if he had any chance
of recovering from his diabetes.

One Sunday we both went to see him in Howrah after a long
bus trip. The moment I saw him I liked him. He had a face I
could trust. He read the horoscope very carefully and for a long
time. At the end he told me that I would have to perform a few
seances to appease a few bad stars that are crossing his cosmic
path right now. He agreed to conduct the *pujās* [worship] for
me. So I visited him three times within a month and spent the
whole day every time. By the end of the last *pujā* he asked me
what was still bothering me. He noticed that I was not happy. He
sounded so sympathetic and kind that I told him all my troubles.
I talked for hours, telling him the story of my life, my father's
house, my marriage, my children, and all my disappointments in
them. By the time I finished talking, I was exhausted; I felt
relieved and as if I had found a "friend"—a "home"—in him. It
did not matter to me anymore if my husband recovered, or if my
sons needed me anymore. I wished to become his disciple right
then. And, ever since, I have been visiting him twice a week. It is
a long distance, I need to change the bus three times, and it takes
about two hours to get to *bābā's āsram*. But once I am there and
near him all my tiredness and pains from the journey go away.
How I wish I could be near him every day and be able to serve
him, attend to his needs, cook for him, and nurse him when he
is ill. . . . I brought some water where he dipped his toes for me
and every morning I begin my day by drinking a sip of it. When I
say my daily prayer to the god, I see his face in my mind and I
know the god is listening to me. . . . My life has changed since I
became his disciple. I am happy now.

The two cases I present here have similarities in the sense that
both women not only chose this alternative rather than the first
one, but also derived great satisfaction from it. This is because of
their family backgrounds and personality structures. In either
case, even if the woman wished to become a powerful figure in
her family, the composition and the condition of the family

made it rather meaningless. Also, the tradition in both families facilitated this choice. The fact that both women had rather quiet and resigned mothers-in-law precluded any pressure on the daughters-in-law to achieve such power. In both cases, the absence of the husbands' attention and the physical absence or ailment of the husband helped to create the sense of helplessness in the women concerned.

These two alternatives aside, a woman may choose both roles, and many do. In situations where the pressure of a large family demands a powerful woman, a woman at this age (forty to fifty) may decide to spend a great deal of time being the matriarch and yet become the disciple of a *guru*, although in such cases the woman may not have such a strong need to visit him and totally depend on him. She may have an absolute limitation of time to begin with. She may devote herself rather casually to worshiping the *guru* as she does her household deities and may give lip-service to her daily prayers. This is done, I suspect, more for the social opinion (it is desirable to become religious at this age) than from personal need. Such women may take a trip or two every year with a group of other elderly matron-mothers to visit the pilgrim centers all over India. Taking trips to places such as Benares, Gaya, Hardwar, or the Kanyā Kumārikā in the south also carries prestige that only wealthy familes can afford. If a woman can take a trip like this, she reaps, apart from her religious duties or satisfaction, the satisfaction that relatives and neighbors look up to her as a fortunate woman whose husband and sons spare her the money to do so.

If a woman lives beyond sixty, she may again become involved in the world of her household. Physically, she is not very able to take much responsibility. This time she offers her services to her grandchildren mostly. She becomes their companion and enjoys telling them tales and stories from holy books and from her own life. She begins to count her numbered days to go to him, the god who is the ultimate destination of everyone and whom she has been seeking many times in her life—in a husband and in a *guru*. This is a stage when she is almost beyond the feelings of frustration. She is resigned to her roles as a woman. She is now an old woman, a grandmother who is there to die. [5]

The Widow

A word must be said about the widowed woman in this section of society. A widow has a choice of going back to her natal family or of remaining with her husband's family. If a woman becomes widowed within a short time of her marriage and has no children, she is most likely to be permitted to go back to her natal family and spend the rest of her life getting involved in her brothers' households. There, if she is fortunate, her sisters-in-law may treat her with sympathy and respect. But more often than not she is considered an extra burden until she becomes old enough to help in the family with her advice and services. If the widow remains in her father-in-law's household, she spends a very awkward ten to twenty years before she is elderly enough to find status in the family. During this period her status as an unproductive woman (the remarriage of widows is not practiced in this part of the country, with very few exceptions) is very precarious indeed. She is polluted because she has no husband and she is not included in any festivals or ceremonies. She is not only a marginal entity, she is of no use to her family. She has to live very quietly behind the scenes, and sometimes she may become the victim of the sexual desire of her brothers-in-law or she may just become involved with one of them. But normally she may be pushed to justify her existence by becoming a glorified maid in the joint-family. By the time she is fifty, she may attain some status for the first time in her married life. Even though she cannot be a fulfilled matron-mother, she may advise and counsel the family in certain matters. Her importance at this stage is more for her services. Now she may be treated like a respectable nurse and service woman to attend the sick and the old. She is also expected to devote most of her time to religious activities, no matter what age she is. Consequently, a widow may plunge into the total religious preoccupation of worshiping a *guru*. The reasons and conditions that attract her toward a *guru* are even more understandable. A widow with children may have a little more respectable status as a "mother," though an unfortunate one.

It is not rare that some of these families in upper-class Bengal often have one or two widows, because of the great age difference between the husband and wife in this section of society. Some of them may be quite powerful and may command great respect when they are older. Some of them remain very quiet and liminal, spending most of their time worshiping their *gurus* and feeling self-pity for their misfortune. Thus, a widow's life in such households goes through frustrations similar to those of her married counterpart, except that her frustrations are more pronounced and deeper.

This brings me to the end of the ontogenetic development of a Bengali upper-class woman, from her childhood through her marriage and into her old age. I hope I have succeeded in demonstrating how a woman is socialized into accepting a number of cultural ideals as her expected roles and how she copes with real-life roles that do not totally correspond with her expectations.

5 Conclusions

A woman in upper-class Bengali society, socialized to certain expectations about married life, is frustrated by it. All the same, society makes available to her a number of compensatory roles for partial and indirect satisfaction throughout her life.

Here I propose to demonstrate (1) how an integrative process between the structural, cultural, and psychological dimensions goes on in a woman's life cycle to give rise to the situation above; and (2) the discrepancies and/or consistencies that occur between her ideal role-interaction and her real-life experience.

Therefore, there are two dimensions to this matrix; the first is the various parallel levels of factors influencing the woman's personality and her expectations; the second is the processual scale of her life cycle divided by various roles, where such expectations are tested in real life situations (see chart, pp. 150–55). In order to demonstrate this, I shall abstract the conceptual frame that emerges from the information and analysis elaborated in previous chapters, by taking the following steps: (a) in this conceptual frame I shall specify the ideal behavior of a particular dyadic role

Configuration of Structural, Cultural, and Psychological Aspects of a Woman's Life

Dyadic Roles and Kin Terms	Affective and Cognitive Content of Dyads	
	ideal	real
Father—Daughter *Bābā—Meye*	$D \longrightarrow F$ Respect, obedience, dependence, affection $F \longrightarrow D$ Respect, obedience, nurturance, indulgence	$D \longrightarrow F$ Same + companionship, friendship, nurturance (in adolescence) $F \longrightarrow D$ Same + companionship, friendship, dependence (later)
Father-figures—Daughter-figure	Same	Same
Daughter—Mother and Mother-figures *Meye—Mā*	$D \longrightarrow M$ Respect, obedience $M \longrightarrow D$ Care, nurturance, covert affection	$D \longrightarrow M$ Same + a tinge of competitiveness $M \longrightarrow D$ Same + a tinge of resentment and jealousy
Wife (New)—Husband *Natun bau—bar*	$(N)W \longrightarrow H$ Respect, love, worship, obedience, fidelity $H \longrightarrow W$ Affection, love, respect	$(N)W \longrightarrow H$ Respect, obedience, with some fear due to distance $H \longrightarrow W$ Ambivalence, some intrigue, sex object
Wife (after the son is born)—Husband *Cheler mā—swāmi*	$W \longrightarrow H$ Same as $(N)W$ $H \longrightarrow W$ Same as $(N)W$	$W \longrightarrow H$ Same + less distance and less fear $H \longrightarrow W$ Affection and some companionship

| Religious Ideals | | Secular Ideals and Parallels |
mythology	mass media	in Literature
Umā, Gouri (child *Durgā*)	*Kumāri brata, Śiva-rātrir brata*	*Kanya* and *Śakuntala* in *Kālidāsa*
Same		
None		Many in modern literature
Pārvati/Śiva Rādhā/Krishna	Musicals, operas, devotional songs, wandering *vaisnavis*	Sitā, Sāvitri the epics. "Laws of Manu." Modern: suffering heroines. Same in movies and other mass media
Numerous *bratas* on ritual levels only	Operas, musicals, songs, plays, movies	Some in modern literature (parallel)

Configuration of Structural, Cultural, and Psychological Aspects of a Woman's Life (*Continued*)

Dyadic Roles and Kin Terms	Affective and Cognitive Content of Dyads	
	ideal	**real**
Daughter-in-law— Father-in-law *Boumā—sasur*	$D\text{-}in\text{-}l \longrightarrow F\text{-}in\text{-}l$ Like a daughter + some avoidance $F\text{-}in\text{-}l \longrightarrow D\text{-}in\text{-}l$ Like a father + some distance	$D\text{-}in\text{-}l \longrightarrow F\text{-}in\text{-}l$ Respect, sense of duty, some avoidance $F\text{-}in\text{-}l \longrightarrow D\text{-}in\text{-}l$ Some dependence + distance
Sister-in-law—Older brothers-in-law *Boumā—bhāsur*	$S\text{-}in\text{-}l \longrightarrow Obr\text{-}in\text{-}l$ Same as d-in-law + more avoidance $Obr\text{-}in\text{-}l \longrightarrow S\text{-}in\text{-}l$ Same as f-in-l + more distance	Same as ideal
Sister-in-law—Younger brother-in-law *Boudi—debar*	$S\text{-}in\text{-}l \longrightarrow Ybr\text{-}in\text{-}l$ Like younger brother, affection + some distance $Ybr\text{-}in\text{-}l \longrightarrow S\text{-}in\text{-}l$ Like older sister and mother, respect, affection	$S\text{-}in\text{-}l \longrightarrow Ybr\text{-}in\text{-}l$ Affection, romantic love, friendship, companionship $Ybr\text{-}in\text{-}l \longrightarrow S\text{-}in\text{-}l$ Love, friendship, adoration, respect
Daughter-in-law— Mother-in-law and other sisters-in-law *Bauma—Sāsuri, Jā*	$D\text{-}in\text{-}l \longrightarrow M\text{-}in\text{-}l$ Obedience, respect, treatment like own mother $M\text{-}in\text{-}l \longrightarrow D\text{-}in\text{-}l$ Treatment like daughter, affection, authority	$D\text{-}in\text{-}l \longrightarrow M\text{-}in\text{-}l$ Obedience, covert conflict and jealousy, sometimes cordiality $M\text{-}in\text{-}l \longrightarrow D\text{-}in\text{-}l$ Some affection, cordiality, covert resentment
Mother—Son *Mā—Chele*	$M \longrightarrow S$ Affection, dedication, nurturance, sacrifice, tolerance $S \longrightarrow M$ Affection, dependence, respect, worship, obedience	$M \longrightarrow S$ Same + more involvement and dedication $S \longrightarrow M$ Dependence, affection, respect, expectations

Religious Ideals		Secular Ideals and Parallels
mythology	mass media	in Literature
	Same as above	A few in modern literature (parallel)
Some *bratas*		
None	None	A few parallel in modern literature
None	None	Epical—Sitā/Lakshmna. "Laws of Manu." Parallel in modern literature
None	Some *brata*	Epical—none. Modern— many. Folk—many
Durgā/Kāli nurturance aspect more than power	*Sasthi* and many *bratas* for the welfare of the son	Epical—Kunti, Gāndhāri. Modern and all mass media —many ideals + parallels

Configuration of Structural, Cultural, and Psychological Aspects of a Woman's Life (*Continued*)

Dyadic Roles and Kin Terms	Affective and Cognitive Content of Dyads	
	ideal	real
Matron-mother—the family *Ginni-mā—paribār*	$MM \longrightarrow Family$ Nurturance, affection, sacrifice, guidance *Family* $\longrightarrow MM$ Respect, dependence	$MM \longrightarrow Family$ Same + some power *Family* $\longrightarrow MM$ Same + some fear
Grandmother—Grandchildren *Thakur mā—Nāti/ Nātni*	$Gm \longrightarrow Gch$ Affection, companionship, friendship $Gch \longrightarrow Gm$ Affection, companionship, friendship	$Gm \longrightarrow Gch$ Same as ideal $Gch \longrightarrow Gm$ Same as ideal
Disciple—Guru *Sisyā—Guru*	$D \longrightarrow G$ Respect, dedication, obedience, dependence $G \longrightarrow D$ Affection, guidance, authority, nurturance	$D \longrightarrow G$ Dedication, love, dependence, obedience, affection, nurturance $G \longrightarrow D$ Acceptance of D's total need to "give"; guidance, affection, attention

Religious Ideals		Secular Ideals and Parallels
mythology	mass media	in Literature
Durgā/Kāli (the aspect power and fear)	Same as above	Modern—some parallels
None	None	Modern—some parallels
No model, but the practice is highly commended in religion		Epical—ideal for men disciples. "Laws of Manu." Modern—casual mention as parallel

and the real-life experience, thus indicating the discrepancy and/or correspondence between the ideal and the real; (b) the factors imbedded in structural, cultural, and psychological realms will be incorporated in the discussion. The integrative process of these factors influences real-life experience to a great extent and the discrepancy or the correspondence between the ideal and the real may occur.

Steps (a) and (b) should show the resultant ratio between the woman's expectations and satisfaction on the emotional level. Therefore, going back to the hypothesis mentioned at the outset, such an analysis seems essential before we can grasp the complexity of the situation.

To begin with, in chapter 2, I discussed the childhood socialization and the adolescent years of a girl just before she is ready to be married. This is a very crucial stage in the formation of human personality in any culture. In the case of a Bengali girl, the first glaring fact is that her childhood training lies in two nearly contradictory worlds, the female and the male. She plays the role of a daughter (*meye*) vis-à-vis her mother and mother figures as well as vis-à-vis her father and father-figures. The cultural norm that defines such dyadic roles has the following ideal.

Daughter-Mother

She must respect and obey her mother and mother-figures (paternal aunts, older classificatory siblings) while listening to what they instruct her about her future life—her role as a married woman. The mother-figures, on the other hand, must give her such instruction through direct verbal communications and by subjecting her to observation of ritual and religious rites, by talking to her about ideal women in the myths and epics, and, of course, by letting her observe and participate in the operation of the family. They should offer her affection and care, but not overt indulgence so that the appropriate seriousness of the message will not be lost.

Daughter-Father

The daughter also must obey the father and father-figures (paternal uncles, older classificatory brothers, male teachers at school, the male music tutor) who give her instruction in schoolwork, in music, and in introducing her to the world of literature, imagination, and introspection. In this case, she is permitted to ask for indulgence through their affection and she demands overt demonstration of their affection. The father figures can offer her indulgence mixed with adoration while giving her instructions, and at the same time act as the counter-vailing aspect to the relatively strict women's world when she is punished or criticized. The cultural ideal in this case is supported by the religious ideal based on the Hindu myth of Durgā who, as a little girl Umā, was loved and adored by her father, the king, and his subjects. Every girl in her father's home should be treated as Umā, soon to leave for her husband's house.

The reality. In real life the ideal behavior between the daughter and the mother and mother figures corresponds well with her actual behavior. Because of the disciplinary and authoritative nature of this relationship, although she does not reap a lot of emotional satisfaction, she finds it less difficult to abide by such normative behavior, partly because of her opportunities to escape into the other world offered by her father and father-figures. The desire on the part of a little girl to be treated with more overt affection than restraint is fulfilled by the latter. As a result, the ideal that prescribes an indulgent behavior between the daughter and the father becomes well attuned to her psychological needs. She, as the ideal goes, may even demand such indulgence and receive it, because the father is supposed to offer her adoration and affection. What really happens is that her interaction with her father as a little girl fails to generate the adoration the myth stresses, but a very relaxed, indulgent relationship does grow and later evolves into friendly companionship. For the father (and father-figures) she is the only female figure who is allowed to be close physically and emotionally, according to familial norms. Thus, while the ideal ignores the girl's adolescence in her father's home (perhaps because of the custom of child-marriage in the past), in real life her relationship with her father and father-figures develops into a very warm and close one. While the daughter makes use of the indulgence offered by the father by enjoying it and perhaps demanding more when she is a child, in her adolescence she begins to offer the same indulgence and affection to the father. The role is somewhat reversed, although the relationship at this stage remains basically a symmetrical one—friendship and companionship with a strong sense of nurturance and dependence from either side.

Let me summarize the additional cultural and structural factors that reinforce the above expectations that result from (1) the gap between her experience with the women's world as opposed to the men's world and (2) the difference between the ideal role and the real experience, especially in the case of her adolescent years with her father.

Her attraction for her father is increased by the fact that the female world tries to interfere with the relationship. The mother and the grandmother voice criticism of her spending time with her father over books and schoolwork. The father also supports her when she is punished by the mother for committing a wrong.

Her knowledge about the very special kind of physical relationship between her mother and father, while it disturbs her and makes her jealous, increases her affection for the father, who is physically unattainable. The knowledge of her imminent departure for her *sasur-bāri* (father-in-law's house), which is also stressed in literature, intensifies the bond.

The daughter observes that whereas her father's relationship to her involves expressed feelings of various kinds, his relationship with her mother, his wife, appears distant and vague. For her, his wife, he appears like the god Śiva—the withdrawn, distant figure, who is considered the ideal husband in Bengali religious mythology. She is attracted to him and thinks that this is the kind of husband that she should have, as the Śiva myth stresses.

While her observations of her parents may puzzle her, they do not leave much impression because she begins to learn of romantic love through her reading and such other sources as friends of her own age. Her tender adolescence, so far protected by the father's love and companionship, receives both information and misinformation, which in turn help her to build up an added element to reinforce her already formed expectation, namely romantic love with her husband, the only man with whom she is socially permitted to experience a full-fledged love relationship. At this stage, she fails to resolve the problem about the dissimilarity that appear to exist between Rādhā and Krishna and her parents. The first tinge of love (*prem*) that she begins to feel quite strongly, she hopes to realize in her marriage—since this is the only possible way open to her. This is that romantic love that her childhood memories of fairy tales, stories of her friends, the poetry and classics that her father and her schoolteachers explained to her day after day, the movies, and precocious schoolmates brought to her. How much her adoration for her father is mingled with her romantic feelings is illustrated very vividly by one case study (pp. 63–64, chap. 2).

The result. Thus, the relationship in her early years of life offers a total emotional satisfaction. Her expectations for her crucial future relationship, namely her husband, is formed on this foundation. These expectations may include the following:

emotional protection and support against the disciplinary and harsh world;
indulgence in affection and love, creating confidence and a sense of security;
nurturance as well as dependence, creating companionship and friendship.

The emotional satisfaction that the women's world fails to offer is accepted and perhaps overcompensated by the men's world. This generates certain expectations about the future.

Wife-Husband

The second structural role the woman has to play is that of a wife, preceded by a short period as a bride only during the period of the wedding ceremony. She also has several roles vis-à-vis the different roles in the family. These roles are the product of pairs of dyadic relations inside the family. For example, in addition to being a new wife to her husband, she is also a daughter-in-law vis-à-vis her father-in-law and mother-in-law. She is a sister-in-law vis-à-vis her husband's brothers, sister, and brothers' wives, and so on. I shall describe all these dyads and their ideal as well as real behavior below.

The ideal. The wife must consider the husband as her god whom she worships as she worshiped the god Śiva in her *Śiva-rātrir brata*. She must obey his wishes without question. She must love and respect him irrespective of his behavior and without the expectation of any return of love and respect from him. The cultural ideal of this relationship is portrayed by such characters as Sitā, Sāvitri, and Behulā. She must follow him in every way and sacrifice her own interests and life if necessary to insure his safety and well-being. She must also be chaste and faithful.

As for the husband, ideal behavior must include affection, love, and respect for his wife, as Śiva had for Pārvati and Satyavān had for Sāvitri. But like Rāma, the hero of *The Rāmāyana*, a man first must be a good and pious son before he considers his wife's welfare. [1]

The reality. It is clear that, without even considering the wife's expectations, the reality will always fall short of the ideal summarized above, because obviously such abstract ideals do not take into consideration the process of the evolution of a relationship. Since the relationship must change and adjust in keeping with changing age and status in the family (especially in interaction with other members), there are bound to be certain problems. In this case the reality looms large in its difference from the ideal, mainly because of the expectations the wife learns to nurture in her childhood relationship with the father. Later the ideals from the epics regarding the good wife have also been complemented and often heavily reinforced by other kinds of cultural, as well as religious, influences, tinting expectations with romantic colors. Let me also refer to the discussion elaborated in chapter 2 on the conflicting image that a woman in this culture is given to internalize regarding the man to whom she is married. Along with the message she receives from the rite *Śiva-rātrir* *brata* to wish for a husband like the god Śiva, she also learns to worship and adore Krishna, the god-lover whose adulterous love for Rādhā is exalted in Vaishnava literature. Both Vaishnava and modern Bengali literature abound in themes of romantic love between man and woman both inside and outside marriage. Modern literature, however, also reflects the reality by indicating the failure of a woman's life when she does expect a romantically exalting marriage. Modern heroines are often torn between their social roles and their romantic desires for personal fulfillment. In addition to this, she is also exposed to western literature and mass media (both western and local) that talk about the intrigue of such love repeatedly and incessantly.

Because of her limited interaction with her husband, she considers him a distant figure of respect to be obeyed and perhaps to be feared a little. The husband treats her as a newly acquired possession to be enjoyed sexually for a while. He has a sense of pride and satisfaction from the fact that he owns a woman who is ready to fulfill his wishes. Basically, there is a lack of communication at the early stage of their marriage that changes into a relationship of some affection and respect later when the wife becomes the mother and the matron-mother.

Let's have a closer look at both the structural and cultural conditions responsible for the intensification of the romantic aspect of her expectations regarding her relationship with her husband as well as the failure to realize such expectations.

During the wedding ceremony, the separation of the girl from her father through the ritualized pathos of the Hindu wedding rite *dān* (father giving away the daughter to the husband) vividly symbolizes in her mind her departure from her natal home—her father's world. This sadness at the moment can only be tolerated by the expectation she nurtures about the man her father gave her to, her husband. She both consciously and unconsciously hopes to replace the father with the husband. This expectation is, however, highly charged with the anticipated tension and thrill about her first sexual experience with her husband-lover, as Rādhā experienced with Krishna—an experience she could not have with her father, the Śiva whom she adored. For her husband, on the other hand, the wedding does not come with the rainbow colors of fantasy and romance. This is because in this patrilineal, patrilocal marriage system, the husband, unlike the wife, is not physically alienated from his family, especially not from his mother—the nurturing and loving figure in his life. Also, the romantic element of his expectation is minimized because of his already internalized attitude toward sex and women (see chap. 3).

The structural situation of subtle censorship against close husband-wife interaction in the family creates a practical condition that does not allow for the formation of a close relationship between the newly married couple. The husband is not encouraged by the family to demonstrate overt affection, if any, toward his wife and son. It is considered shameful to be overtly attentive to one's wife in such a household.

The result. The gap between the woman's expectation and what her marriage has to offer becomes very clear within a short time of her marriage, and she discovers that her husband offers only perhaps the social image of a distant, protective figure. Even if he felt any emotional closeness toward her, in their formal interaction that remains unexpressed. As a result the correspondence between the expectations founded on the father-daughter relationship and intensified by other enculturating factors and the realization remains very low indeed. A woman's acute disappointment in her sexual-emotional life with her husband is clearly stated in a number of case studies. One woman confesses, "I missed my father, who discussed his office problems with me. . . . I began to feel I was not at all as important to my husband as I was to my father or even to my older brothers". (chap. 3, pp. 98–99).

Daughter-in-law–Father-in-law

The ideal. Ideally, a daughter-in-law in this section of Bengali society should behave like a daughter to her father-in-law as well as to her older brothers-in-law, although she must maintain a physical distance according to the rule of avoidance. For example, she ought not to address them directly, talk to them only when asked by them, and she must look after their practical needs and comforts only when commanded or requested to do so by them or by older female relatives. Thus, her normative behavior toward her older male relatives is meant to be categorized as her "duty" rather than something she likes to do. While the ideal of behaving like a daughter is verbalized, no one bothers to see that it really happens on both behavioral as well as psychological levels, as long as the daughter-in-law continues to fulfill her duties ungrudgingly. And the same applies to the other side of the dyad where ideal role vis-à-vis the new daughter-in-law is supposed to be like that to her father.

The reality. She observes her duties by carrying out the jobs she is asked to perform for the father-in-law and the older brothers-in-law, such as attending to their meals, baths, afternoon naps, and so on. She does these without much pleasure or grudge because doing these makes her a good daughter-in-law. She just abides by the norm not to create any adverse familial opinion.

The result. Because of this behavior in actual life, her father-in-law does not become a father figure for her. Such a relationship (like father-daughter) is only possible if she has been brought up over years in close contact with the father-in-law. Therefore, despite the term *bābā* she uses for him, he fails to give her the satisfaction that came from her father as a nurturant as well as a dependent figure. Her relationship with her older brothers-in-law is even more distant because the rule of avoidance operates more strictly in this relationship, and also because these men do not have as much need for her in their daily lives. They have their mother, sisters, and perhaps daughters to fulfill such needs. So they also fail to offer the emotional substitution for the father and brothers in her natal home.

Female Relatives

Her actual relationship with her female relatives seems to correspond well with the social and cultural ideals except in the case of the husband's mother and a sister-in-law in case the husband is close to them. In other words, the tension in her relationship with the women is directly proportional to the closeness of the women and her husband. Conversely, the quality of the relationship between the woman and her female relatives may have very little repercussion on her relationship with her husband. She may decide independently to maintain (if she is clever enough) a cordiality with her mother-in-law and sisters-in-law, using tact and diplomacy, just because it reduces the possibilities of additional tension in joint living.

The condition of her husband's closeness with his mother and sisters-in-law in the family is structurally given with possible variations due to accidental factors such as the number of sons the mother has and the personalities of the sisters-in-law. The woman's frustrations from unrealized expectations with her husband may be said only to be aggravated by this structural situation.

Sister-in-law—Younger Brother-in-law

The ideal. This relationship is ideally that of an older sister and a younger brother. [2] The religious parallel idealizing this relationship comes from the epic *The Rāmāyana* where Lakshmana, Rāma's younger brother who, like Sitā, followed him into exile, treated his sister-in-law Sitā as a respected mother. Sitā, on the other hand, treated Lakshmana like a son or a younger brother, i.e., with affection only. There must also be a subtle avoidance in this relationship from both sides. The social norm in Bengali culture, however, allows an open and intimate friendship to grow between a *boudi* and a *debar* without romantic content. According to this norm, he can offer her the emotional satisfaction that her classificatory brothers offered her in her father's home while she offers him a friendship his classificatory sisters ought to offer him as well. The *debar* is the only male figure with whom familial custom allows to grow an open and intimate relationship.

The reality. Permitted by the norm, she finds her *debar* the only person who comes close to satisfying her desire for a close companionship with her husband, with the clear possibility of having friendship in return. She spends a lot of time being his secret confidante and feeling very happy in such a close friendship that comes to have a strong romantic overtone. The structural and psychological factors that enhance the growth of this relationship (both affection and romantic love) are as follows.

Unlike her relationship with her older male relatives, there is no definite duty prescribed for a *boudi* to perform for her *debar*. Her freedom to interact with him as she likes is a structurally given condition.

Also given by the cultural norm is the sanction against a complete sexual intimacy, and this knowledge on the part of both *boudi* and *debar* encourages them to have a romantically charged, intimate friendship (although in a very few cases the relationship becomes an intense, but short-lived, sexual one).

The *debar*, because of his own position in the joint-family (see chap. 3), needs to offer as well as to respond to her approaches in a relationship that substitutes for her relationship with her husband.

The result. As a result there develops a relationship that offers the woman indirect emotional protection (due to the love and adoration that the *debar* offers her), creating some confidence and a sense of partial security and companionship and friendship (arising from the dependence the *debar* has on her nurturance). But although this relationship offers this partial satisfaction, it does not offer total gratification because the *debar* does not offer her the indulgence and nurturance she had from her father. Second, because of the mixed asexual nature of the relationship, her fulfillment in romantic expectations remains only partly realized.

The next chronological phase in her status in her *sasur-bāri* includes the roles of a mother, a matron-mother, and a grandmother.

Mother-Son

The ideal. The mother must give affection, care, and total nurturance along with adoration to her son. She must be ready to make any kind of sacrifice for his welfare and well-being. This cultural ideal has its parallel in religion as depicted by the mythology of Gopāl, the child Krishna whom his mother Jashodā worshiped. Many Bengali mothers have little brass figurines of Gopāl in their household shrines, and mothers may even nickname the newborn babies Gopāl. There are numerous folk proverbs, songs, stories, and tales to reiterate the theme of the glory that a woman achieves by being a mother and one who sacrifices for her son. The epical characters such as Kunti, Gāndhāri, and others from medieval and modern literature encourage a woman to respect this ideal of motherhood.

The son, on the other hand, must also worship, respect, and love his mother as his first and foremost obligation and duty. He must also give her care in her old age, especially in the absence of his father.

The reality. In actual life, at the first stage of her motherhood, a woman becomes extremely involved with her newborn son. She gives her total affection and care to the son because she is grateful for his birth, which, overnight, has changed her status in the family. Because of her idea that a woman is happy when she has a son, she invests her emotions in this relationship. Her constant physical and emotional contact with her son at this early stage helps to build up a very close relationship. As the son grows to adolescence and adulthood, the picture begins to change for her. The son, who as a child offered her satisfaction by his passive acceptance of her affection and dedication, does not depend on her totally. He has sisters, sisters-in-law, and his friends on whom to depend. While he shows respect to his mother and still depends upon her, he does not feel any obligation to return to the same extent his mother's devotion and affection.

The strucural and cultural factors that support and enhance this reality may be summarized as follows. In his early years a son is encouraged to depend on the mother totally. The custom of exclusive sleeping arrangement with the mother (or mother figures), lack of physical and emotional contact with the father because of the familial sanction against over demonstration of affection toward his wife and son, the practice of late weaning[3] all enhance his dependence on his mother's love, thereby accentuating the mother's expectations for the future.

The fact that the social structure and the cultural norm always emphasize the asymmetrical aspect of the relationship between the mother and the son (namely the mother must sacrifice for the son, at least until the mother is old and incapacitated) gives the son little obligation to return the mother's devotion and affection. The security of mother's love is taken for granted.

The cultural norm does not prepare either the mother or the son for the implications of the mother-son relationship. Neither the mother nor the son is clearly made to believe that sooner or later the mother must release the son, emotionally and physically, to allow him to become an adult. The situation is aggravated by the joint-living where the mother remains in the same household with the son throughout her life. This continued living together with the mother, unlike the situation of a woman who is separated from her parents by the rule of patrilocal residence in marriage, becomes very crucial in the acceleration of the mother's frustration because the son is given opportunities to realize his emotional needs (generated by his intense childhood experience with his mother) by other women within the joint-family. In a sense, unlike his wife's situation, this opportunity has more potential because in his case he has developed a relationship with his sisters and sisters-in-law over the years. The duties and obligations are often founded on emotion. Therefore, paradoxically, from the mother's point of view, her continued presence in his life, where other women are also present to offer him emotional satisfaction, acts against her own interests.

Cultural and religious factors in the formation of the son's personality encourage him to internalize the concept of the mother-goddess, which splits the image of a woman into a mother and a sex-object in his concepts and attitudes (see chaps. 2 and 3). He must seek satisfaction of a romantic-sexual kind elsewhere. He tries to solve this problem of dividing his attention and need between women occupying different relationships by complementing the mother with the others (wife, sister, sister-in-law), thereby increasing the mother's frustrations.

The result. Thus the satisfaction a woman derives when she gives birth to a son (reinforced by her inflated self-image as a mother) and continues to derive by giving the child her complete attention, devotion, and affection begins to wane when the son is grown. Her frustrations from the unrealized expectations in this case seem to be a direct result of the gap between the promise offered by her experience as a new mother and reality as she grows older. The period of the satisfaction from motherhood and her interaction with the young son may be prolonged in the case of some women, if they are psychologically suited to accept and enjoy the role of a matron-mother. Here her sense of power and authority may be a substitute for the need for love. This may happen only if she already has the temperament for such a role and faces challenges in the household that require her to become not only a matron-mother but a matriarch. And yet very few women are successful in drawing complete satisfaction from such a role since it does not offer them their need for dependence.

Thus the failure to replace her father with her husband or with a combination of other male relatives in her *sasur-bāri* (though temporarily buried under the satisfaction of motherhood, which offers her a chance to give rather than receive) accelerates her frustrations to the point where her last attempt is almost desperate. This time she seeks compensation in a relationship outside the family, where every man has deluded her. She finds a *guru*.

Guru-Disciple (*Sisyā*)

The ideal. This relationship, being extrafamilial, is not founded on strict familial norms and ideals. The ideal is, however, a religious and cultural one in the broad sense of the term. (This cultural ideal has its roots in the classical notion of the relationship between a teacher and a student, essentially of a superior and subordinate nature.) The ideal behavior for the disciple is the same for both male and female. A disciple should address a *guru* as *bābā* (father) and treat him respectfully and with utter obedience; the *guru* must treat the disciple with affection, guidance, and understanding. [4] He must be strong enough to accept the demand of the disciple for total nurturance; he should always be prepared to accept the total dependence of the disciple. He becomes not just a religious teacher, but a guide, a friend, and a father to the disciple because he is guiding the disciple to be with the god and attain ultimate salvation.

The reality. The above ideal symbolizing *guru-sisyā* behavior suits the need of a Bengali woman perfectly. In her declining years (often near menopause) she craves to become an infant as well as the young girl she was with her father. She wishes to go back to her early, blissful childhood and happy adolescence. She attempts to recapture this fantasy by becoming a child-woman to her *guru*, whom she calls *bābā* and to whom she stresses her utter helplessness as well as her love and devotion, just as Rādhā offered the same to Krishna, her god-lover. She gives herself totally. It is a total abandonment, a giving of herself with all the affective content that she has learned to give but found she could not give because no man in her family ever possessed or offered such a total image. The *guru* accepts all this with grace.

The structural (not familial) and cultural norm elaborated below adds to the condition in such a way that a successful relationship from the woman's point of view is almost predefined.

It is considered extremely commendable for a woman of middle age to become a *sisyā* of a *guru* and devote her time to religious activities. The members of the immediate family also support this norm because, by being involved with a *guru*, a woman in her middle age reduces the possibilities of her remaining overly involved in the household and "getting in everybody's way." The conscious rationale is that a religious woman always brings prestige to the family. The vital psychological factor is the need of the woman to have a total relationship with her *guru*. She not only need have no qualms but also receives overt encouragement. The fact that the *guru* is a man (and often quite young—mid-forties—and quite attractive) and one who is outside the orbit of kinsmen makes it easier for her to build up a total relationship that is not in conflict with any particular role-image such as father, brother, or husband.

The *guru's* association with the Vaishnava cult and the literature in which he is particularly well-versed and his frequent use of the love theme of Rādhā-Krishna in his talks and sermons to his disciples make it easier for the woman to identify him with god Krishna, who is also a god of love. She can relate to him, at least in her fantasy, as Rādhā related to Krishna. This identification is also helped by the insistence in the Vaishnava cult that every worshiper (male or female) must try to identify with Rādhā completely (*Rādhā bhav*) in order to succeed in feeling total devotion (*bhakti*) to Krishna, the god.

The result. Her relationship with the *guru* at last comes close to the fulfillment of her craving for a father figure who is also a combination of the Śiva and Krishna images.

Grandmother-Grandchildren

If a woman lives beyond sixty and is not totally satisfied with her *guru* she may try to find some solace in her close companionship with her grandchildren.

The ideal. Ideally this relationship is very cordial and sweet. The grandmother's only obligation is to enjoy the frolic of the grandchildren and offer emotional support to them when they (especially the male ones) need protection from the discipline of their father and their uncles. They must treat her with respect and cordiality.

The reality. The real situation corresponds fairly well with the ideal because other factors do not interfere with this relationship, which is marginal anyway. There are no unfulfilled expectations to create tension. The above analysis shows that the developmental process of a woman's interactions with members of her family results in an accelerated frustration unless she accepts the last compensatory role with her *guru*, which appears to offer most satisfaction.

One point that emerges from this study is pertinent to the system called the joint-family. It is noticed that the woman finds the most satisfactory compensatory role outside the confines of her joint-family, in which she tried and failed to realize complete satisfaction. It appears that in the structure of the joint-family system a role that combines the ideal elements of both the father and the *guru* role is not feasible. It seems that the familial roles within the process of the developmental cycle of the joint-family are such that psychological fulfillment remains only partial. Thus all the roles serve to maintain the structure of the joint-family.

To elaborate, it seems that in order to maintain a system like the joint-family individuals must be capable of adjusting to their own roles and to others both as role-occupiers and individuals (with idiosyncratic needs) so that conflict can be avoided. The possibility of such conflicts is inherent in the system because individual personality needs sometimes conflict with the need of the whole system. Needs may be generated indirectly and enhanced by other sociocultural factors, as we have seen already. For example, a woman's psychological needs are generated by her early childhood experience in her natal home, and her interaction with her father and brothers has a strong emotional content that develops over time. Consequently, the roles and the individuals become somewhat fused for her. The adjustment between her personality and the role, say, of her father, becomes less difficult. In her husband's household, where she is introduced to the various roles as an adult, the individuals and the role-actors are not fused for her because emotional dependence is missing. Her crucial role in her husband's joint-family, "the wife," is not a continuation of her childhood experience. She must make new adjustments to the role of her husband as well as to her husband as an individual. The formal aspect of role inter-action may work fairly well if she is given some time to learn to adjust, provided her expectations in the natal home do not interfere. Abstractly put, from the point of view of the mainte-nance of the joint-family system, so long as she makes the successful adjustment to the role "husband" (and, for that matter, all other roles) the threat of disruption does not arise. But the real picture is slightly more complicated, because a role-occupier is also a human being with individual needs that the system generates indirectly.

The only way this problem can be handled (from the point of view of the system) is to offer every individual member possibili-ties for partial satisfaction from each role to fulfill these needs while the system is permitted to continue unchanged. For the woman to receive total or close to total satisfaction, therefore, she has to seek a relationship outside the system since the joint-family cannot permit total satisfaction to one individual at the cost of rendering insignificant the needs and satisfactions of the other members.

This kind of situation is inherent in the structure of a joint-family and also exists for a male who does not leave his natal home. In the case of the wife, this society with its patrilocal marriage rule alienating her from her natal home aggravates the situation by intensifying her psychological needs.

This study brings out another fact in the realm of culture and personality. An individual's personality and expectations are not shaped solely by religio-cultural ideology but are also circumscribed by a very concrete set of socio-familial customs and code of behavior. This, in turn, influences thought processes and feelings, some of which are reflected in behavior and are verbalized, some of which are merely felt, and some of which remain unconscious. Hence the analyst has to take cognizance of various levels in human interaction that are determined by personality structure as well as social customs. In a culture where roles are well defined and the individual is expected to remain within socially prescribed and sanctioned roles, the culture may also provide ways to fulfill psychological needs that are indirectly generated and reinforced.

In a culture that does not hand down the same religio-cultural ideologies that influence the fantasy level of personality, or does not strictly maintain the socio-familial behavioral norms and codes, such an approach may not be useful. For example, within Bengali culture those parts of the society that are directly affected by such changes as the political partition of the country resulting in forced displacement of families and individuals may not exhibit the pattern that emerges in this study. Comparative research between two such sections of Bengali society might highlight the areas in an individual's life where the seeds of frustrations and possibilities of satisfactions are hidden. Such a finding might be used for wider research in other cultures as well.

Afterword

Two decades have passed since the first writing of this book. During this time some changes which have direct bearings on women's lives have taken place in Bengali society and culture. Although the original research was done over a decade, between the late fifties and the late sixties, a somewhat static picture had emerged, because the women I studied lived rather secluded lives. The information on early socialization received from their recapitulated life histories and my own observations of young girls did not seem to be noticeably affected by the external changes. Nor were there evident any significant changes in the behavior of their daughters and granddaughters during the time of my research. In this economic group (upper and upper-middle class) external changes, such as women entering professions, happened slowly. Only now are there several discernible changes.

The political partition of Bengal in 1947 had brought with it a major demographic change resulting from rapid migrations of a sizable Hindu population from the eastern part, which in turn had a disastrous economic effect. Even the upper class families experienced an unprecedented decline in their wealth and income. Therefore, joint families became economically unviable.

Break-up of the joint family had by far the most significant impact not so much on the socialization as on the expectations of all its members. Young men began to relocate, sometimes outside the country, in search of jobs. Girls learned early that education and professional skill would be required to survive before and after marriage. By necessity young women began to be educated with professional goals. Women no longer could remain entirely as "ladies of leisure." In fact, in marriage negotiations, whether arranged by the families or by the young couples themselves, the working women became the most desirable choice.

The second phenomenon that emerged from this hard economic reality was a group of single women, some of whom remained unmarried to support their families and some of whom were divorced.

Although divorce became legal in India in the 1950s, only the decades of the seventies and the eighties saw a small group of upper and upper-middle class Bengali women daring to consider this option. With the changed cultural expectation that a woman needs to earn a living alongside with men, she is also exposed to newer ideas and possibilities and is now capable of realizing it.

These changes have been compounded by the additional factor of increasing Westernization of the American brand through travels and television via the satellite. Many households have sons or relatives in America who travel back and forth bringing American values of consumerism as well as equality and individualism.

A model of a new woman is being reinforced by the current women's magazines and journals and by an evolving mass media, especially television, now widely available in these households. She is economically independent and stands up for her rights within and outside the family. She is self-aware and ready to fight to become man's equal, and she strives to become that "woman" who will bridge the age-old gap between the respected figure and the sex-object (pages 117–21).

Whatever this transformed woman may look like on the pages of women's magazines or the television screen, in reality she is something like the following.

She may be in her twenties or thirties, unmarried or married, and she is responsible for the care of her elderly parents and young siblings or of her children and husband. If lucky, she may have part-time household help. Her daily routine begins early in the morning, preparing the breakfast and the family for work and school, taking the children to school or to a school bus stop, then struggling through a crowded bus on the way to her own work. Returning in the evening on another crowded bus, she stops at the market to pick up fresh fish and vegetables for the evening meal. On weekends she may enjoy socializing with her husband and friends or relatives, which means that she prepares snacks and numerous cups of tea for the guests.

Although sympathetic to his wife's plight, the husband is not used to the idea of helping her in household chores. In this culture it is not yet expected of him. The same man, however, may even learn how to cook if he is in a foreign country!

The question can be raised if this scenario along with other external changes predict a growingly discontented group of women who are likely to launch a feminist revolution eventually. Before one can answer that, we need to look at the psychological changes within the woman herself and at her relationships both inside and outside the family. We need to discern how changeable her internalized religious and cultural ideals are, and more importantly, whether these newfound advantages are (in her eyes) worthy of exchange for the old compensations which are still offered by the culture? In other words, is she prepared to sacrifice the rewards of the role of the "good wife/mother," therefore, the "good woman," by rebelling against the old system of the division of labor as well as against other situations within the family?

Let us look at some of the changed roles in a woman's life. The nature of her socialization has not changed that much except that in everyday interactions she has fewer father figures. Her relationship to her father is still very close. She is, however, also more aware of her mother's hardship and may even feel an identity with her as a growing woman. The two worlds of women and men are no longer that separate, and her mother is not just one among several other women relatives. She does not need to flee to the "father's world" to escape the harsh and disciplinary world of women. She learns early that women all over the world are going through a movement of liberation and justifiably so.

Her education is definitely more westernized, with more emphasis on English, science, and physical fitness than on classics and religion. She is no longer as exposed to the household deities and rituals, although the mass media still continues to offer some of the traditional values and images. The romantic input comes more from modern literature and movies which use realistic problems of sociology than from imaginative rendition of mythology. In many of these plots women are not only objects of romantic desires and dreams but also victims of men's aggression and power, although celebration of good family relations and motherhood still continue to be an important part of the media message.

Marriage no longer is the only option that a young Bengali woman looks forward to. Since she is expected to train for a salaried profession, she now has time and opportunity to know men outside her family. Even working married women can build either romantic or friendly relationships with colleagues. Psychologically, these men may replace the brother-in-law of the joint family and to some extent the husband who may not be available yet for an open companionship. She tries to emulate the "new woman" of the magazine or the cousin who lives in America. Some married women may even indulge in extramarital affairs; others may form groups where they can talk about their problems with their husbands and families.

The husband's connection to his family, especially his connection to his mother, can still be of major concern for the young wife in these nuclear families. Because of the relatively recentness of separate living arrangements, the son appears to be even more conscious of his duties and obligations toward his parents. He tries to compensate by being overtly attentive, through either financial help or visits to the parents. The mother, who was brought up by the old system and expectations, has a hard time adjusting to this physical distance from her son. She, of course, blames the daughter-in-law, who in her eyes is being modern and selfish.

In one of my most recent visits to Calcutta, I met a highly educated woman, a retired professor, who told me that she was willing to give her son a major part of her hard-earned savings for him to go abroad provided he did not take his wife with him. She supported her position by adding "No wife can ever love her husband as deeply as his mother loves him." The deep bond and emotional dependency between the Bengali mother and her son are strong enough for even an educated woman to voice such blatant prejudice.

From the son's point of view, this dependency makes him feel responsible for the mother's happiness albeit he is well aware of the manipulative aspect of this expectation. In today's nuclear household a wife is liable to confront her husband with this issue and they may even have an open discussion on it. But the wife also knows that he cannot shake this responsibility off, though he may not be emotionally bound to his mother as much as he would have been in the past. Once the matter is openly discussed, his wife is more tolerant of his position. A common complaint by the modern wives is that the husbands are reluctant to treat the wives as partners or companions with whom they can be open and honest and admit such problems and share their dilemmas.

Whether the case of the retired professor's feelings toward her son is an exceptional one is hard to tell. I hear a lot of gossips about the jealous mothers-in-law and ultramodern, selfish daughters-in-law. Even if the above example is an extreme one, it tells us that external economic and social changes may take generations, if ever, before the emotional texture of relationships will change. Such a change will have to come from the younger generations. In other words, the step toward a healthy emotional separation from the mother will have to be taken by the son. Some men are beginning to do this by speaking up, sometimes to support wives who are contributing to the family income, a contribution that even possessive mothers-in-law have to acknowledge. It is interesting to speculate what kind of mothers-in-law these working, more independent young mothers will make. Only time will tell.

Some of the older mothers who are not as possessive of their sons are taking up voluntary social services, a resurrected tradition of some of the nineteenth-century upper-class women. Newly acquired ideas and visions combined with an erosion of existing religious practices allow some women to break the pattern and go outside the home to help others who are less fortunate. A sense of jealous competition between the two generations of women may contribute to the efforts on the part of the older generation to find engaging alternatives outside the family.

The tradition of devoting oneself to a guru that I observed in my earlier research is waning, at least in the cities. However, a new trend is visible. Young educated wives of the Calcutta business elite are becoming obsessed in following some of the internationally celebrated gurus. Could this group behavior be an unconscious compensation of the denial of the personal involvement with the deity through the personage of the guru? Could this obsession also be a compensation for the increasingly secular, rational, and materialistic life-style that the educated women have consciously embraced in the last two and three decades?

In psychoanalysis it is often observed that obsession as a pathological symptom also masks a genuine spiritual need, the need to connect with the transcendent aspect of life. One thirty-year-old married woman who is also a lecturer in a women's college in a wealthy neighborhood said, "I don't know why, but when I am with the guru I feel a peace of mind I cannot otherwise. I forget that my husband drinks too much and has little time for me." This woman's feelings after being with a guru and perhaps her reasons for seeking such a relationship in the first place are not so different from those of the older generations. Women who can find emotional fulfilment in their work and family life and have intimate relationships with their husbands may not need such a connection.

In my earlier research I observed that the crucial psychological foundation in forming a Bengali woman's expectations in marriage and life were conditioned strongly by the Hindu religious and mythological input in her upbringing. One such symbol was the dichotomous image of the ideal husband and the romantic lover illustrated by the Hindu gods Siva and Krishna respectively. Not only were these images internalized unconsciously by centuries of tradition, but they were also reinforced by the conscious practice of rituals and other instructions. Now that the cultural manifestations of religious mythology are being replaced by more secular messages and Westernized ego ideals, her inner gods are repressed to the deeper unconscious.

Since Sigmund Freud's work with the unconscious nearly a century has passed, and by now depth psychologists have enough experience with the human psyche to know that no repressed material is ever lost. If not allowed expression either in social roles or in creative symbols, it gathers energy in the unconscious creation of "complexes," which then surface in the guise of compensations. Compensations can take the form of obsessions or even of explosive psychotic episodes, or of a massive outburst of irrational excess, as exemplified by extreme fundamentalist movements.

It will be centuries before the internalized images of masculine ideals in the unconscious of the Bengali woman will change. The Siva-

Krishna dichotomy, among other symbols, still exists as an archetypal foundation for a paradigm of a Bengali woman's relationships with men and she will continue, consciously or unconsciously, to strive for its fulfilment.

Manisha Roy

Appendix

Age, Education, and Number of Members of Informants' Families

Informants	Age at the time of interview	Age at marriage	Education final degree rec'd.	age degree rec'd.	No. of children	Age of children at time of interview	No. of joint-family members
1	25	20	B.A.	20	1	3(m)	11
2	25	19	B.A.	19	2	4(m), 2(f)	9
3	28	20	I.A.	18	2	5(m), 3(f)	12
4	28	21	B.A.	21	1	6(m)	10
5	28	20	I.A.	18	3	6(f), 4(m), 2(m)	11
6	28	19	High School	17	2	7(m), 5(m)	9
7	28	18	College, 1 year	17	2	8(m), 5(f)	10
8	28	17	High School	16	3	9(m), 7(m), 5(m)	9
9	29	20	I.A.	19	2	7(m), 3(f)	10
10	29	21	B.A.	21	2	6(m), 3(m)	11
11	29	23	M.A.	23	1	5(m)	8
12	29	24	M.A.	22	1	4(f)	10

13	29	19	B.A.	19	2	8(f), 4(f)	8
14	29	20	B.A.	20	2	8(f), 7(m)	11
15	30	19	I.A.	18	3	9(f), 8(f), 6(m)	12
16	30	21	M.A.	21	1	7(m)	10
17	30	22	One year after B.A.	20	3	7(m), 5(m), 3(m)	12
18	31	23	B.A.	20	2	6(m), 5(f)	10
19	31	20	I.A.	18	3	8(m), 6(m), 4(f)	9
20	32	19	B.A.	19	2	10(f), 8(m)	10
21	32	20	B.A.	20	3	10(f), 8(f), 6(m)	8
22	33	19	B.A.	19	2	12(m), 10(m)	10
23	33	24	M.A.	22	3	8(m), 7(f), 5(f)	9
24	34	20	I.A.	19	4	12(m), 12(m), 8(m), 5(f)	11
25	37	21	B.A.	20	2	15(f), 10(m)	8
26	37	18	High School	17	3	16(f), 15(m), 12(m)	12
27	40	22	B.A.	21	4	16(m), 12(m), 10(m), 8(f)	11
28	41	22	B.A.	21	3	17(f), 15(m), 12(m)	12
29	45	19	I.A.	19	5	20(m), 22(m), 18(f), 16(f), 10(f)	9

Age, Education, and Number of Members of Informants' Families (*Continued*)

Informants	Age at the time of interview	Age at marriage	Education final degree rec'd.	age degree rec'd.	No. of children	Age of children at time of interview	No. of joint-family members
30	45	18	High School	17	3	20(f), 16(f), 14(m)	10
31	46	20	I.A.	19	2	24(m), 20(m)	12
32	47	21	I.A.	20	3	25(f)*, 23(m), 20(m)	9
33	47	19	High School	17	4	27(f)*, 25(f)*, 20(f), 15(m)	9
34	47	18	High School	18	3	26(m), 24(m), 20(m)	10
35	49	21	College, 1 year	18	3	26(m)*, 24(m), 19(f)	8
36	49	19	I.A.	19	4	27(f)*, 25(f)*, 23(m), 20(m)	7
37	49	19	I.A.	18	3	25(f)*, 23(f)*, 20(f)	8
38	50	20	High School	18	5	29(m)*, 27(m)*, 24(m), 22(f), 20(m)	11
39	50	19	I.A.	19	5	28(m)*, 26(f)*, 25(f)*, 23(f)*, 18(m)	7

40	51	21	High School	18	4	27(m), 26(f)*, 24(f)*, 20(f)	10
41	51	21	I.A.	20	4	25(m), 23(m), 20(m), 18(f)	9
42	51	20	I.A.	19	5	30(f)*, 28(f)*, 25(f)*, 24(m), 20(m)	8
43	52	18	High School	17	5	32(m)*, 30(m)*, 28(m)*, 25(f)*, 24(f)*	12
44	52	19	High School	18	4	30(m)*, 29(f)*, 25(f)*, 24(m)	10
45	52	18	High School	16	4	32(f)*, 30(f)*, 25(m), 23(m)	8
46	53	17	High School	17	5	35(f)*, 34(m), 30(f)*, 28(f)*, 22(m)	9
47	53	19	I.A.	18	3	30(m)*, 26(m)*, 20(m)	12
48	53	20	High School	18	2	31(f), 28(m)*	8
49	53	19	I.A.	17	3	30(f)*, 29(f)*, 25(m)	6
50	54	18	I.A.	18	5	35(m)*, 34(m), 33(f)*, 30(f)*, 28(m)*	11

NOTE: Data collected during the period 1965–69.

*Married.

I.A.: (see note on following page).

I.A.: Intermediate Arts degree received after two years of college after ten years of secondary education. The system has been changed in recent years; now a B.A. degree is offered after three years of undergraduate studies in a college which begins after twelve years of high school. In the last column *total number of joint-family members* indicates a fluid number because it changes with the marriages of the girls and some of the male members may go away for jobs or higher education elsewhere for a number of years. Like any other data, the number indicates the exact number at the time of interview. All families have at least one of the parents-in-law living, some have grandchildren, and all with the married men had their nuclear families living with the informant and her husband. Almost all had one or two married and/or unmarried brothers-in-law and/or unmarried sisters-in-law.

All informants were married, with living husbands. The difference in age between spouses was between four and ten years.

Notes

Foreword

1. Sāvitri is the proverbial heroine whose story is told in *The Mahābhārata* III; her goodness and truth were such that she rescued her husband from the hands of Yama, the god of death. Behulā is the heroine of the medieval Bengal *Manasā-mangal*; her devotion was so great that she floated down the river on a raft, her husband's corpse on her lap, until she reached the realm of the gods and persuaded Manasā, goddess of snakes, to restore her husband to life.

2. The text of the *Sasthi-mangal* is available in *Myths and Symbols: Studies in Honor of Mircea Eliade*, ed. J. M. Kitagawa and C. H. Long (Chicago: University of Chicago Press, 1969).

Chapter 1

1. "Bengal" will be used to refer to Hindu West Bengal where the investigation was conducted, although in broad cultural terms West Bengal and Bangladesh (formerly East Pakistan) remain one unit.

2. In Bengal's domestic form of ritual (*brata*), legends, and folktale totems such as "duck," "serpent," "mountains," "riv-

ers," "frogs," and "crocodile" are very common. In secular art and writing these items loom large, as can be seen in later literature (as in Tagore). For a discussion see Sudhansu Kumar Roy, *The Ritual Art of Bratas of Bengal* (Calcutta: Firma K. K. Mukhopadhy, 1961).

3. Sashi Bhusan Chaudhuri, *Ethnic Settlements in Ancient India* (P. I. Northern India, Calcutta General Printers and Publishers Ltd., 1955).

4. *The Mahābhārata* is the largest epic poem in any language, consisting of some 80,000 verses (compiled and written over a period from the fourth century B.C. to the fourth century A.D.), intended to be a treatise on life and its various aspects, including religion, ethics, polity and government, philosophy, and salvation. Although the main theme of the epic is a story based on the rivalry between the cousins of a royal lineage, there are numerous episodes, fables, and myths directly or indirectly connected with the central story that make *The Mahābhārata* a wonderful mine of the history, lore, and mythology of India.

5. The Bengali language evolved about the tenth century, and modern Bengali evolved through three phases: (a) Old Bengali—A.D. 950–1350, (b) Middle Bengali—A.D. 1350–1800, and (c) Modern Bengali—A.D. 1800 onward. See J. C. Ghosh, *Bengali Literature* (London: Oxford University Press, 1948).

6. Vaishnavism: in the fourteenth and fifteenth centuries, a religious movement with strong "romantic" enthusiasm spread all over eastern India, perhaps as a reaction to as well as a result of the "corruption" in Buddhism, the prevalence of the extreme form of Tantrism, the dogmatic rigidity of Brahmanical Hinduism and the impact of Sufi Islam with a strong emotional element of devotion. The movement was characterized by its use of the vernacular languages (as opposed to Sanskrit), rejection of Brahmanical authority as ritual intermediary for worshiping God, and rejection of the hierarchy of the caste system. Strong emphasis is laid on singing and dancing as steps toward ecstatic communion with God. The major theme of the songs came to center around the life and love of Lord Krishna and his consort Rādhā.

7. Tantrism and Sahajiyā: Tantric tradition broadly refers to a non-Vedic ritual system, either Hindu or Buddhist. The subject matter of Tantric literature may include esoteric yoga hymns, rites, magic, and even medicine. The essential element of Tantric thought is that a man is a microcosm containing within himself all the elements of the universe and God. Unlike Brahmanical Hinduism, Tantric tradition includes women as eligible to receive religious teachings, and they can be "gurus" themselves. Devi, the goddess, embodies all women, and all women are worshipful. Sexual rituals have become an important part of some Tantric traditions (for a scholarly discussion see Agehananda Bharati, *The Tantric Tradition* [A Doubleday Anchor Book, 1965]).

Sahajiyā refers to a cult based on a system of worship and beliefs in which the natural qualities of the senses should be used, not denied or suppressed. The origin of the cult perhaps goes back to the eighth or ninth century in Bengal. In Edward C. Dimock's words, "The roots of these Sahajiyā sects lie well within the ancient tradition of the Tāntras. Both Tāntrics and Sahajiyās believe that man is a microcosm, a miniature universe; both believe in unity as the guiding principle of this universe, that all duality, even that of the sexes, is falsehood and delusion and that cosmic unity is regained, or represented, by man and woman in sexual union . . . ; both believe that there should be no caste division among worshippers; . . ." (Edward C. Dimock, Jr., *The Place of the Hidden Moon: Erotic Mysticism in the Vaishnava-Sahajiyā Cult of Bengal* [Chicago: University of Chicago Press, 1966], pp. 35–36).

8. Sashibhusan Dasgupta, *Obscure Religious Cults as Backgrounds of Bengali Literature* (Calcutta: University of Calcutta, 1946).

9. In his play *The Red Oleander*, the character of Bishu is a very good personification of this spirit.

10. See Milton B. Singer and Bernard S. Cohn, eds., *Structure and Change in Indian Society* (Chicago: Aldine Publishing Company, 1968), for discussions on the concepts of Great Tradition and Little Tradition.

11. One of the best examples of such a deity is Sitalā, goddess of smallpox, who is widely worshiped in rural Bengal. Local myths began to form around her during the middle ages and gradually became included in the religious scriptures and texts of Bengal. Her popularity with the villagers, who fear her wrath during the smallpox season, raised her status to the level of local pantheon.

12. For the meaning and implication of the term Sanskritization, please refer to M. N. Srinivas, *Social Change in Modern India* (Berkeley and Los Angeles: University of Caifornia Press, 1969), pp. 1–45.

13. The cult of Satya-Pir represents a god unifying Buddhistic and Islamic traditions. This god is still worshiped by both Hindus and the Muslims in rural Bengal. See Samaren Sen, *The Roots of Bengali Culture* (Calcutta: Eureka Publishers, 1966).

14. In fact, throughout Bengal's history one can trace three centers that gave rise to the efflorescence of the culture at different times. Gaur was the center in north Bengal in the pre-Muslim era, Nadiya was the center of south-central Bengal during the Vaishnava era, and Calcutta in the nineteenth century. It is interesting to note that cultural leadership based on these centers moved from north to south along the river Ganges toward the rich delta economy.

15. For a discussion on *kulinism* see Sankar Sengupta, *A Study of Women of Bengal* (Calcutta: Indian Publications, 1970), pp. 15–16.

16. *Sati*: The word *sati* (also written suttee) literally means "a virtuous

woman," but refers to a practice of self-immolation of wives on their husbands' funeral pyres. This custom (whether widely practiced or not) was first mentioned in a Greek account of Alexander's invasion of India after which time numerous *sati*-stones with inscriptions commemorating the faithful wives following their husbands in death were found all over India. The living cremation of the *sati* was voluntary in theory, but later accounts of the middle ages clearly indicate that family and social pressure made it virtually obligatory among the higher castes. In Bengal during the eighteenth and nineteenth centuries this practice among the upper castes seemed to be wide enough to attract strong criticism from the English rulers and the liberal leaders of the culture.

17. Nirmal Kumar Bose, *Modern Bengal* (Calcutta: Vidyodaya Library Private, Ltd., 1959), pp. 39–40.

18. *The Purānas* (literally meaning "ancient stories") are compendia of legends and religious instructions which date back to the Gupta period of Indian history (A.D. 300–500). Although in their present form with numerous interpolations they do not date far back in history, they deal with very old legendary material connected with episodes about the lives of individual gods such as Vishnu, Śiva, Vāyu, and Bhagavata. Some of these episodes are very popular because of their down-to-earth human quality.

19. The Young Bengal movement was led by a young professor at the Presidency College named Derozio, perhaps one of the most controversial figures in Bengali history. He attracted students with his radical ideas. The group, also known by the name "philosophical rebels," drew their inspiration from the revolutionary tradition of France.

20. During the period from the fourteenth to the seventeenth centuries, a great *bhakti* (dedicated devotion) movement gripped most parts of northern and eastern India. The Bengali Vaishnava poetry represents the way this devotional mood and sentiment found expression in Bengal through the narration of the life and love of Krishna and his consort Rādhā. The peak of such creation was in the sixteenth and seventeenth centuries. The *Bhagavata Purāna*, the basic text of Bengal Vaishnavism written in the ninth or tenth century, depicts two basic themes. One is that separation of lovers is the proper attitude of the worshiper toward God, because it increases the desire for God, the beloved one. Intense and selfless desire for God is the mainstream of Vaishnava religion. Second, to the Vaishnava poets the image of true love and of its extension, extramarital love, which was only an image of love of the human soul for God, can be realized only in separation. Hence the most poignant and appealing section of Bengali Vaishnava poetry expresses the sentiment of Rādhā's burning desire for Krishna, her beloved, who is not always available and faithful to her.

Vaishnava lyrics and poetry are not just limited to the Vaishnava sect, but sung and proudly possessed by all Bengalis. For a thorough and illuminative discussion on Vaishnava poetry and tradition see Edward C. Dimock, Jr., *The Place of the Hidden Moon: Erotic Mysticism in the Vaishnava-Sahajiyā Cult of Bengal* (Chicago: University of Chicago Press, 1966).
21. For reference see J. H. Hutton, *Caste in India: Its Nature, Function and Origin* 3d. ed. (Bombay: Oxford University Press, 1961).
22. The term *Pujā* in Bengal always refers to the great Hindu religio-cultural festival celebrated for four days in autumn when the goddess Durgā is worshiped throughout the whole state and even outside Bengal wherever there is a sizable Bengali population. This festival is considered the most significant in the religious-ritual calendar of Bengal.

Chapter 2

1. Among upper-class and middle-class families in urban and rural India, worry over the dowry for the marriage of the daughters is particularly high. In case of the lower class and caste a girl is not considered such a burden because, unlike her upper-class counterpart, she often provides labor and economic subsidy to the family until she is married. A male child in the upper-class household, on the other hand, promises the future economic asset in terms of his own earning, as well as the dowry that he may bring through his marriage. His sister is never encouraged to take a job, even though she may often be well qualified. She becomes a double burden because in such a household she has to be educated as well as provided with a dowry for the purpose of fetching a good match, which in turn brings prestige and status to her family.
2. In this part of Bengali society, while no conscious method of birth control is practiced, a two to three year spacing between the children is considered proper. There are no available statistics to support this observation. A woman may also have her first two or three children in rapid succession.
3. *Pānchāli* and *brata-kathā*: *Pānchāli* is a story read aloud or told by a priest, priestess, or by an ordinary woman while worshiping a deity to describe the pictorial version of an episode that gave rise to a *brata* or a rite. These verses are usually based on themes of everyday life that a woman experiences and what she should do in order to receive blessings from her deities. Thus the *pānchāli* may dictate the basic duties of a good wife. *Brata-kathā* is similar to *pānchāli* in the sense that the *kathā* (story) narrates the origin of the rites and often justifies their observance. These *bratas* are nothing more than rites replete with certain basic faiths

and beliefs of folk-life translated into rituals that are observed for some material benefit. Women (both married and unmarried) observe these rites for the fulfillment of worldly desires and material prosperity such as the desire to acquire a good husband, sons, wealth, and a happy life.

4. The grandmother usually puts such expressions in a proverbial form such as "*swāmi putrer ghar karte hobe*" ("she will have to make a home for the husband and the son"). Such proverbs and sayings are often used to express the message that a girl's future is only justified if she becomes a homemaker for her husband, sons, and her husband's family. Older women use such proverbs to indicate the ongoing tradition in the thinking of the people.

5. The term *sasur-bāri*, which will be used throughout the book, literally means "the household of the father-in-law." The implication of the term, however, encompasses the whole world that comes with marriage for a woman. Its implications are quite clear in the minds of women when they use the term. Nearly all my informants said to me that if they knew what they had to go through in the *sasur-bāri* they would not have bothered to go to high school and college. All the education they need is to be able to write an occasional letter and be able to read novels. The books at college did not tell them what a good wife and mother should do.

6. Betel-leaf and nut are chewed all over South Asia. The leaf is chewed with pieces of areca nut, a pinch of lime, and other condiments. The juice of the nut is supposed to give a slightly intoxicating effect. Women are found to be addicted to this habit. They chew betel after every meal, especially after a heavy lunch, when they find the juice of the leaf and the nut helps them to relax and doze off for an afternoon nap. The chewing of the betel-leaf and nut also gives the mouth and the lips a red tint, and this, in Bengal, symbolizes a happily married woman, who also uses vermilion in the parting of her hair and wears a red-bordered sari.

7. *The Rāmāyana*, *The Mahābhārata* and *The Purānas* (the Bengali versions) are the books that all households keep and read. The women usually choose particular episodes such as those that stress the glory of the sacrificing wife and mother. They aslo relate the same stories to the little girls.

8. An example, translated by N. C. Chaudhuri in his *Bangalir Jibane Ramani* (Calcutta: Mitra Ghosh, 1970) from Kālidāsa's *Kādambari*, is as follows:

> . . . Stole he my maidenhead,
> And today's husband mine!
> Just the same are nights of Spring

. . . .

Ah! on that very spot for coitus fantasies
Wistful wistful grows the heart.

9. Johann Jakob Meyer, *Sexual Life of Ancient India*, 2 vols. (London: George Routledge & Sons Ltd., 1930), 2:295.

10. Edward C. Dimock, Jr., and Denise Levertov (tr.), *In Praise of Krishna: Songs from the Bengali* (Garden City, N. Y.: A Doubleday Anchor Original, 1967), pp. 8, 17. Also see Romesh Chandra Dutt, *Cultural Heritage of Bengal* (Calcutta: Punthi Pustak [1st ed., 1877], 1962). Also refer to the following for further examples from Vaishnava literature: W. G. Archer (ed.), *Love Songs of Vidyapati*, tr. Deben Bhattacharya (London: Allen & Unwin Ltd., 1963). Deben Bhattacharya (tr.), *Love Songs of Chandidas, the Rebel Poet-Priest of Bengal* (London: Allen & Unwin Ltd., 1967).

11. I once watched an audience in a huge park in the central section of Calcutta where a popular company was staging such an opera. In the audience, which numbered several thousand, were a great many women of different ages. By the time the play reached its climax, the women were carried away with so much emotion that at the end many ran toward the stage in order to touch the feet of the actor who played the role of Krishna. This outburst of mob-ecstasy that I watched in 1965 reminded me of a similar scene in Central Park in New York City in 1962 when Elvis Presley was chased by screaming and shrieking girls.

12. See Wendy D. O'Flaherty, "Asceticism and Sexuality in the Mythology of Siva," *History of Religion* 8 (1968–69): 300–37; 9 (1969–70): 1–41.

13. The devotional songs (*bhajan*) a girl is encouraged to learn serve several purposes. She can entertain her older relatives by singing them. Old people like to listen to such songs sung by a girl they are fond of. The family also feels that by learning such songs and by singing them to herself and others, the girl cannot escape the devotional impact that such songs impart. A good woman should be religious and devoted to God. Furthermore, these kinds of songs are considered appropriate for a bride-to-be to sing when the prospective bridegroom's family comes to interview her. The older people of the bridegroom's family are especially impressed by such performance, which indicates not only the girl's talent as a singer, but also the taste and attitude of her family, which encouraged her to learn such songs rather than modern songs. The most common theme in these *bhajans* is that of a woman devotee from West India, Meera Bāi, who dedicated her life to her god, Krishna. She sings songs directly to her god and lord with whom she wishes to be united so that she can attain ultimate salvation. For example, a common line that is repeated in most of such songs goes like this: "Meera, the servant of her master and lord, wishes to offer herself to him."

14. Tagore's songs, which he composed music for (about a thousand), are very popular in Bengali society, and it is respectable for every educated Bengali girl to know how to sing them. There are music schools all over Calcutta and other towns that girls attend once or twice a week for two to three years; there they learn how to sing such songs and some even receive degrees conferred by the university for this kind of music alone. These songs are included in public recitals, music conferences, radio broadcasts, and movies. Adolescents learn them, memorize them, hum them to themselves, and quote them while writing letters or school essays.

15. The term "cultural function" (the English term is used) refers to cultural performances at schools and colleges two or three times a year on occasions such as "foundation day," the beginning of a long vacation, and so on. The program of such "cultural functions" consists of musical recitals, dance-dramas, and plays written by Tagore and a few other modern authors. Tagore's music and plays, especially his dance-dramas, which are based on episodes from the epics, are used repeatedly for such cultural functions.

16. Chitrāngadā is the title role of a dance-drama written and composed by Tagore. The theme is based on the story of love between Arjuna, one of the heroes in *The Mahābhārata*, and Chitrāngadā, an ugly princess. She was transformed into a beautiful woman (Surupā) by the god of love, Madan, so that Arjuna could be won over. The dance-drama weaves together the theme of Chitrāngadā's pain and despair as an ugly woman in love and her hope and pleasure as a transformed beauty.

17. The professions of music, dancing, and acting are not considered very respectable and desirable by Bengali society, though talent in all girls in such areas of the fine arts is encouraged by families, schools, and society at large. Ability to perform in "cultural functions" is considered part of the girl's qualifications as a well-bred, well-educated woman, but these abilities are of secondary importance in her ultimate and only role—a married woman and mother. Only women who have no stable and protective families enter such professions to earn their living because they have no other alternatives.

18. The selection of these pieces seems to be arbitrary. The educational system selects them primarily for the literary style and because they represent a particular time of history. Such curricula were seldom changed up until the independence of the country, when a revision was necessary because of public opinon against including English as the major second language in Indian educational systems.

19. For elaborate discussion supporting this statement refer to Sushil

Kumar De, *History of Bengali Literature in the Nineteenth Century*, 2d ed. (Calcutta: University of Calcutta Press, 1919).

20. For a critical evaluation of Bankim Chandra Chatterjee see Sunil Kumar Banerjee, *Bankim Chandra: A Study of His Craft* (Calcutta: Firma K. L. Mukhopadhyay, 1968).

21. This is not to claim that classical Sanskrit literature does not deal with a kind of romantic love that Kālidāsa and Bhababhuti so exquisitely create. More examples of such expression of love can be given from Sanskrit love poetry of early Tamil and South Indian literature. What makes the situation in Bengal noteworthy is that in the nineteenth century a new wave of consciousness regarding a kind of romantic love (that consists of devotion and a sophisticated expression of aesthetics) between men and women was felt. Romantic love existed not just among the epical and religious figures who belonged to an early era and a different world. However, this transformation of setting and characters took time.

22. Nirad C. Chaudhuri, *Bangalir Jibane Ramani* (Calcutta: Mitra and Ghosh, 1970).

23. Examples of using natural imagery for beauty and other concepts of women (mother) abound in Bengali literature, from Kālidāsa to Rabindranath Tagore. Kālidāsa used imagery and similes such as clouds, rains, rivers, and vines to indicate the different moods of women. Vaishnava poetry uses water, fields, and the earth to describe Rādhā in various moods. I give a few examples from Tagore.

> There comes the morning with the
> Golden basket in her right hand
> Bearing the wealth of beauty,
> Silently to crown the earth. (*Gitanjali*)

> Infinite wealth is not yours,
> My patient and dusky mother
> Dust.... I have seen your tender face
> And I love your mournful dust,
> Mother Earth.... ("The Gardener")

24. *Kapalakundala* (1866) by Bankim Chandra tells the story of a woman in the wild setting of deltaic Bengal where the thick forests skirted by the thin beaches like a sari-border become one with the woman herself. The analogy seems possible only when the woman is completely identified with the natural beauty.

25. For support of this statement refer to Sunil Kumar Banerjee, *Bankim Chandra: A Study of His Craft* (Calcutta: Firma K. L. Mukhopadhyay, 1968), and Sushil Kumar De, *History of Bengali*

Literature in the Nineteenth Century, 2d ed. (Calcutta: University of Calcutta Press, 1919).

26. It is interesting to note, however, that the most significant character that Tagore created to personify this combined image is a woman (in his long short story "Laboratory") who comes from northwest India, not Bengal. Perhaps Tagore was a bit hesitant to destroy the Bengali image of a woman who is either a mother or a sex object.

27. The only example I can find, like every other aspect of life, is in Tagore's writing. His short story, "The Devotee" (in *The House-warming and Other Selected Writings*, Amiya Chakravarty, ed., Mary Lago and Tarun Gupta, tr. [New York, Toronto: New American Library, 1965]), deals with a woman's irrational devotion to the author, whom she treats as a *guru*, a representative of her god.

28. This particular journal, which became extremely popular during the fifties and early sixties, ceased in the late sixties. Most of my forty- to fifty-year-old informants either subscribed to it or borrowed it from their friends. The movie journals, however, always flourish and are extremely popular among women of all ages and adolescents of both sexes. Interestingly enough, a number of well-known writers contribute to these journals, and this ensures their wide readership.

29. Most junior and high schools in Bengal are not coeducational. The students experience the coeducational atmosphere only at the very beginning (nursery level) and at the very end (university level) of their student life. Bengali society feels that during their formative years boys and girls must be segregated. These schools and colleges, however, employ male teachers to teach girls and sometimes female teachers to teach boys. Consequently, many girl students may have strong sexual fantasies about young male teachers. Some girls hero-worship them almost openly.

30. The name *battolā* refers to proscribed pornography written in an earthy, colloquial Bengali and including vulgar illustrations. The word *battolā* literally means "under the banyan tree." Evidently, these books used to be sold by roadside vendors in the shade of a banyan tree where they could easily pack up their merchandise quickly if the police spotted them.

31. *Jhāl muri* is a Bengali word referring to puffed rice with hot pepper and other condiments. Girls and young boys in school and colleges buy them from vendors during their recess periods and eat them as snacks while chatting and gossiping.

32. In this part of Bengali society a young girl (as the case study shows) usually learns about menstruation from her peers. It is rare that a mother or an aunt explains the whole matter to a girl approaching puberty. The subject matter, like the subject of sex, is considered taboo.

The notion of pollution connected with menstruation (as in some other parts of India) is not very clear. In some families, if there is an orthodox mother-in-law alive and if there is more than one daughter-in-law, a menstruating daughter-in-law may not perform the duty of worshiping the household deity. Since in these households cooking is usually done by hired cooks, any taboo in that area is not observable. It seems to me that while there exists a general sense of pollution in the minds of women, particularly the older women, the observance of the taboo is not as strict as it is among rural families or in other parts of India.

33. The Bengali word *prem* may be translated as "romantic love." It has elements of both sexual love and such other feelings as affection, respect, companionship, and friendship. Usually the word is used to indicate love between a devotee and his or her god.

34. Uttam Kumar is the most popular movie star in Bengal among women from ten to sixty. He is the Rudolph Valentino of all seasons in Bengal.

35. A very apt example of this may be found in the well-known close relationship that India's prime minister Indira Gandhi had with her father, Jawaharlal Nehru. Mrs. Gandhi was not only an intellectual and political disciple of her father, but she accompanied him all his life. Her apprenticeship as a politican began early as a result of her close association with her father.

36. "Who can predict a woman's moods?" is a free rendering of a very commonly used Sanskrit proverb referring to a woman's mind, which is "*Debā no jānanti kuto Manushyā?*" i.e., "That which even the Gods do not know, how can men figure out?"

Chapter 3

1. Good omens, *sulakkhan*, refer to a few culturally acceptable signs a bride or a girl from a respectable family should have. While no one is very clear about the exact nature of these signs, they all talk about them and cover the following points. A girl with good omens must have certain physical endowments such as fair complexion, sharp nose, long black hair, black eyes, shapely body with graceful carriage, and light, small feet, a small and low forehead. She must also be gentle-voiced and gentle-mannered and keep her eyes downcast when encountering men and elders.

2. See Sastibrata Chatterjee, *My God Died Young* (New York: Harper and Row, 1968), for a very good example of such an interview. Similar

descriptions may be found in several short stories written by Tagore, including "Samapti."

3. "Feminine customs" is a loose translation of the Bengali *stri āchār*, meaning certain customary rites that only women participate in during a wedding or some kind of festive occasion. In a wedding, these rites emphasize through the use of symbolic songs, proverbs, and games the bride's future role as a wife in her husband's family. These are designed to allow the newly married couple to get acquainted with each other. One such game is a mock dice game played by the couple immediately after the wedding in which the women help the girl to win and let the bridegroom alone only after he promises acceptable gifts for the bride in the future.

4. The Bengali *bier jal* literally means "water of marriage," which metaphorically alludes to cohabitation. Men use this crude term often among close friends to mean depositing semen inside the wife.

5. The man continues to join his peers for gossip as he did in his bachelor days. See the case study on pp. 102–3. He may also visit some friends and their families where he already has built up close friendship with a friend's wife.

6. Married young men studying in foreign countries for higher degrees often indulge in affairs with foreign women because of the opportunities in such cultures of free mixing. This is not hard for him to rationalize because, usually, he has a double standard about the women he can desire and enjoy and the women he can marry and respect. The foreign women, or most of them, fall into the first category, namely, the object of desire. A number of male Indian students on American campuses told me, "These American girls are good to have sex with, but one cannot marry them. They are no good for marriage."

7. Mother-in-law–daughter-in-law relationships in this part of Bengali culture are not one of stereotypical, overt conflict. The conflict is often subtle and the relationship may even appear quite friendly and cordial. See chap. 5 for more on this.

8. Good looks are important to a girl because families of the upper class and caste wish to maintain such physical endowments in future generations. Also, they think it important for the girls to be beautiful and aesthetically presentable. Men do not have to be good-looking, so long as they are well-educated and are well-established in their professions. Families with ugly girls have great difficulty in finding husbands and often a high dowry may be needed to solve this problem.

9. Nirad C. Chaudhuri, *Bāngālir Jibane Ramani* (Calcutta: Mitra and Ghosh, 1970), pp. 98–100.

10. The literature, as well as the press of the time (late nineteenth and early twentieth century), abounds with examples of such episodes where

young and middle-aged wives of landlords or their descendants had no alternative but to be sacrificing wives. A very good example can be found in the novel by Bimal Mitra entitled *Saheb, Bibi, Golam* (Calcutta: New Age Publishers, 1957–61).

11. Wendy D. O'Flaherty, "Asceticism and Sexuality in the Mythology of Siva," *History of Religion* 8 (1968–69): 300–37; 9 (1969–70): 1–41.

12. G. Morris Carstairs, *The Twice Born: A Study of a Community of High Caste Hindus* (Bloomington: Indiana University Press, 1967). In this connection, although Carstairs' general contention regarding some aspects of Hindu male personality is supported by my observation in upper-class Bengal, let me hasten to add that his study disregards the female point of view altogether. As a result we really have an utterly one-sided view. It would have been interesting to know what the feminine reaction to such an attitude (as he describes) is like. Does it continue to reinforce the male attitude he describes? In my own study, obviously within a joint-family, there are other sociological factors that bear upon such male attitudes. Carstairs also fails to elaborate on the social and cultural factors that may have added explanations for the attitude of his Rajput male informants. His interpretation of the goddess-worship seems somewhat similar to what I observed in Bengal, although the ambivalence that a Bengali man nurtures toward Kāli, a goddess he adores as well as fears, is not well spelled out in Carstairs' interpretation.

13. The social approval for the open practice of prostitution is on the wane. Modern Bengal has changed its attitude regarding sex and women since the idea of the new romanticism found roots in this culture around 1850. However, the practice is still quite common, although the open practice may not be approved. Consequently, it is carried out with a great degree of secrecy.

14. The Bengali proverb "*mā howā ki mukher kathā!*" means "Motherhood is more than just a word." There are numerous proverbs and sayings constantly repeated by older women that imply that to become a mother requires a lot of hard work and only a few very fortunate women have the good luck to be good mothers.

Chapter 4

1. There is no formalized period for such taboos in this part of the culture. If the woman goes to her father's house to have the child, she may remain there five to six months. If she is in her husband's house she

is considered in a polluted state for at least a month and sleeps alone with the child. After a month, even though sleeping with the husband is not encouraged, in reality it may take place. It is extremely difficult to have data on this. Nobody wishes to talk about such matters.

2. This kind of conjugal love is often devoid of erotic and romantic contents. The concept of conjugal love in Bengal as it evolved through the centuries starting with the Vedic era has always had the problem of incorporating the erotic-romantic as well as the respect-affection aspects of the relationship. The ideal of conjugal love illustrated by the epic and legendary figures such as Sitā and Sāvitri usually incorporates the romantic content to a great extent. However, in the real family situation, although the emotional aspect (affection and respect) are not underrated, the romantic-erotic aspect is definitely underplayed. Please see chap. 3 and chap. 4 for more on this.

3. Suniti Kumar Chatterji, *In Memoriam Kamala Devi, 1900–1964: A Husband's Offering of Love and Respect* (Calcutta, 1965).

4. This desire is often articulated by very old women who put it the following way: "All I am counting are days for being one with him, my *debatā* [god]. The *samsār* [household world] disgusts me. The sooner I can reach him, the better."

5. Some grandmothers after the age of sixty or so may absorb themselves totally in the companionship of the grandchildren if they are physically active and emotionally suited. Their need for a regressive childlike desire may thus be fulfilled to some extent. They identify with the grandchildren. Even the kin terms used by the grandmother for her grandsons and granddaughters are the same as used by the siblings among themselves.

Chapter 5

1. For the ideal behavior of husband, wife, and other members of the joint-family see "The Laws of Manu" in *Selected Books of the East*, edited by Max Müller (Delhi: Motilal Banarsidass, 1967), 25:327–29.

2. In *The Rāmāyana* the duties of the husband's younger brother toward his elder brother's wife is elaborated. Lakshmaṇa, Rāma's brother, who accompanied Rāma and Sitā during their forest exile of twelve years, followed the rules of ideal behavior. For instance, the brother-in-law never stared at his sister-in-law's body or looked above her feet, the dust of which he must touch to his head to show his respect for her. He must always treat her as his mother. See "The Laws of Manu," p. 337, on this behavior.

3. There is no available data on the practice of weaning. No woman is clear on this. The time of weaning varies between two to three years after the birth of the child. This period may be cut short by the arrival of another child. Women feel rather flexible and relaxed about this. There is no familial sanction attached to either weaning early or late.

4. For *guru-sisya* behavior see "The Laws of Manu."

References

Bengali and Sanskrit Sources

Bhāgavata Purāna. Murshidabad edition. 5 vols. Behampur: Rādhāraman Press, 1924 B.S.

Chaudhuri, Nirad C. *Bangalir Jibane Ramani*. Calcutta: Mitra and Ghosh, 1970.

Dasgupta, Sasibhusan. *Sriradhar Kramavikasa—darsane o sahitye*. Calcutta: E. Mukherji, 1953.

Manasā-Vijaya of Vipra-dasa. Edited by Sukumar Sen. Calcutta: Asiatic Society of Bengal, 1953.

Sen, Sukumar. *Bangalar Sahityer Itihasa*. 3 vols. Calcutta: Modern Book Agency, 1940.

Srikrisna-Kirtana. Attributed to Badu Chandidāsa. Edited by Vasataranjan Ray. Calcutta: Bangiya Sahitya Parisad, 1323 B.S.

Thakur, Abanindranath. *Bangalar Brata*. 2d ed. Calcutta: Kantik Press, 1944.

Vaishnava-granthabali. Edited by Satyendranath Basu. Calcutta: Basumati Sahitya Mandir, 1342 B.S.

Vaishnava-padavali. Edited by Sukumar Sen. New Delhi: Sahitya Akademi, 1957.

English Sources

Articles

Bagchi, Prabodh Chandra. "Development of Religious Ideas." In *History of*

Bengal, vol. 1. Edited by R. C. Majumdar. 2 vols. Dacca: Dacca University Press, 1942.

O'Flaherty, Wendy D. "Asceticism and Sexuality in the Mythology of Śiva." *History of Religion* 8 (1968–1969): 300–37; 9 (1969–1970): 1–41.

Leach, E. R. "Caste in Modern India and Other Essays." *The British Journal of Sociology* 14 (1963): 377–78.

Sarma, Jyotirmoyee. "Formal and Informal Relations in the Hindu Joint Household of Bengal." *Man in India* 31 (1951): 51–71.

Srinivas, M. N. "Some Thoughts on the Study of One's Own Society." In *Social Change in Modern India*, pp. 147–63. Berkeley: University of California Press, 1969.

Books

Archer, W. G., ed. *Love Songs of Vidyapati*. Translated by Deben Bhattacharya. London: Allen & Unwin Ltd., 1963.

Bhattacharya, Deben, tr. *Love Songs of Chandidas, the Rebel Poet-Priest of Bengal*. London: Allen & Unwin Ltd., 1967.

Banerjee, Sunil Kumar. *Bankim Chandra: A Study of His Craft*. Calcutta: Firma K. L. Mukhopadhyay, 1968.

Bose, Manindra Mohan. *The Post Chaitnya Sahajiya Cult of Bengal*. Calcutta: University of Calcutta Press, 1930.

Bose, Nimai Sadhan. *The Indian Awakening and Bengal*. Calcutta: Firma K. L. Mukhopadhyay, 1969.

Bose, Nirmal Kumar. *Modern Bengal*. Calcutta: Vidyodaya Library Private, Ltd., 1959.

Carstairs, G. Morris. *The Twice Born: A Study of a Community of High-Caste Hindus*. Bloomington: Indiana University Press, 1967.

_____. *The Autobiography of an Unknown Indian*. New York: Macmillan Company, 1951.

Chaudhuri, Sashi Bhusan. *Ethnic Settlements in Ancient India: Part 1, Northern India*. Calcutta: General Printers and Publishers, Ltd., 1955.

Chatterjee, Bankim Chandra. *Indira and Other Stories*. Translated by J. D. Anderson. Calcutta: Modern Review Office, 1918.

_____. *Kapalkundala*. Translated by Miriam S. Knight. London, 1845.

_____. *The Poison Tree*. Translated by Miriam S. Knight. London: T. Fisher Unwin, 1884.

_____. *Sitaram*. Translated by S. C. Mukherjee. Calcutta: R. Cambray and Co., 1903.

Chatterjee, Sarat Chandra. *Kironmoyee—Charitraheen*. Translated by Benoy Lal Chatterjee. Bombay, Calcutta: Jaico Publishing House, 1962.

Chatterjee, Sastibrata. *My God Died Young*. New York: Harper and Row, 1968.

Chatterji, Suniti Kumar. *In Memoriam Kamala Devi, 1900-1964: A Husband's Offering of Love and Respect*. Calcutta, 1965.

Chattopadhyay, Gautam, ed. *Awakening in Bengal*. Calcutta: Progressive Publishers, 1965.

Coomerswamy, Ananda K. *The Dance of Shiva*. New York: Noonday Press, 1957.

Das, S. R. *Folk Religion of Bengal*. Part 1, no. 1. Calcutta: S. C. Kar, 1953.

Dasgupta, Surendranath. *A History of Indian Philosophy*. 5 vols. Cambridge: Cambridge University Press, 1951-62.

————. *Obscure Religious Cults as Backgrounds of Bengali Literature*. Calcutta: University of Calcutta Press, 1946.

De, Sushil Kumar. *Early History of the Vaishnava Faith and Movement in Bengal*. Calcutta: General Printers and Publishers, 1942.

————. *History of Bengali Literature in the Nineteenth Century*. 2d ed. Calcutta: University of Calcutta Press, 1919.

De Rougemont, Denis. *Love in the Western World*. New York: Doubleday, 1956.

Dimock, Edward C., Jr. *The Place of the Hidden Moon: Erotic Mysticism in the Vaishnava-Sahijya Cult of Bengal*. Chicago: University of Chicago Press, 1966.

————. *The Thief of Love: Bengali Tales from Court and Village*. Chicago: University of Chicago Press, 1966.

Dutt, Romesh Chandra. *Cultural Heritage of Bengal*. Calcutta: Punthi Pustak, 1877, 1962.

Ghosh, J. C. *Bengali Literature*. Oxford: Oxford University Press, 1949.

Hopkins, Thomas J. "Vaishnava Bhakti Movement in the Bhagavata Purāna." Ph.D. diss., Yale University, 1960.

Hutton, J. H. *Caste in India: Its Nature, Function, and Origin*. 3d ed. Bombay: Oxford University Press, 1961.

Jung, Carl G. *Psychology and Religion, East and West*. Collected *Works*, vol. 11. New York: Pantheon Books, 1958.

Karve, Iravati. *Kinship Organization in India*. Decan College Monograph Series, no. 11. Poona: Decan College, 1953.

Kennedy, Melville. *The Chaitanya Movement: A Study of the Vaishnavism of Bengal*. Calcutta: Association Press, 1925.

Koph, David. *British Orientalism and the Bengal Renaissance: The Dynamics of Indian Modernization, 1773-1835*. Berkeley: University of California Press, 1960.

Long, James. *Oriental Proverbs in Their Relation to Folklore, History, Sociology with Suggestions for their Collection, Interpretation and Publication*. Calcutta: Jatya Sahitya Parisad, 1875, 1956.

Majumdar, Ramesh Chandra, ed. *History of Bengal.* Vol. 1. Dacca: Dacca University Press, 1942.

Mehta, Rama. *The Western Educated Hindu Woman.* Bombay: Asia Publishing House, 1970.

Meyer, Johann Jakob. *Sexual Life of Ancient India.* Vol. 2. London: Routledge & Sons, Ltd., 1930.

Müller, Max. *Selected Books of the East.* Vol. 25. Delhi: Motilal Banarsidass, 1967.

Rahim, M. A. *Social and Cultural History of Bengal.* Karchi: Pakistan Historical Society, 1963.

Roy, Samaren. *The Roots of Bengali Culture.* Calcutta: Eureka Publishers, 1966.

Roy, Sudhansu Kumar. *The Ritual Art of Bratas of Bengal.* Calcutta: Firma K. L. Mukhopadhyay, 1961.

Sen, Dinesh Chandra. *History of Bengali Language and Literature.* 2d. ed. Calcutta: University of Calcutta Press, 1954.

Sengupta, Sankar. *A Study of Women of Bengal.* Calcutta: Indian Publications, 1970.

Singer, Milton B., ed. *Krishna: Myths, Rites, and Attitudes.* Honolulu: East-West Center Press, 1965.

Singer, Milton B., and Cohn, Bernard S., eds. *Structure and Change in Indian Society.* Chicago: Aldine Publishing Company, 1968.

Srinivas, M. N. *Social Change in Modern India.* Berkeley: University of California Press, 1969.

Tagore, Rabindranath. *The Housewarming and Other Selected Writings.* Edited by Amiya Chakravarty; translated by Mary Lago, Tarun Gupta. New York and Toronto: New American Library, Signet Classic, 1965.

Thompson, Edward J., and Spencer, A. M., trans. *Bengali Religious Lyrics, Shakta.* Calcutta: Association Press, 1923.

Index

The photographs are courtesy of Marta
Nicholas and Manisha Roy.

The title page photograph is of a conch shell,
whose sound marks the daily life of each Hindu
Bengali household as well as religious events
and special occasions. The figure of Kālī, one
of the fiercer forms of the goddess, was carved
on the shell by Aśvinī Nandī.